Hope for A Troubled Heart

Wes Belfrey

Published by Belfrey Books

Copyright © 2014 by Wes Belfrey

all rights reserved,

No part of this publication may be reproduced, distributed, or transmitted in any form or by any means, without the prior written permission of the publisher, except in the case of brief quotations embodied in critical reviews and certain other noncommercial uses permitted by copyright law.

First Belfrey Books Edition 2014

For information address:

BELFREY BOOKS

275 East 4th Street Suite 400
Saint Paul, MN. 55101

Printed in the United States of America

Publisher's Cataloging-in-Publication data
Belfrey, Wes

Hope For A Troubled Heart
p. cm.

ISBN 978-0-9836504-2-3

Dedication

To my precious mother, Frances Louise
To my lovely wife, Delores and to my children
Dionne, Christine and Christopher

In Loving Memory

*My dad the late Elder Wesley Belfrey, Sr.
My little sister Darilyn Belfrey.*

Acknowledgements

First and foremost I would like to thank My Lord Jesus Christ, without whom I could do nothing. My sincerest thanks to Christine & Nathan Johnson, Debbie Gorman, Oksana Klimok, Michelle Mann, Dana Grilauskas, Dina Tarasov, Violet Limkov, Queen Esther Wade and all the family of Integrated Nursing and Model Health Care. Thank you all for your great advice and insight, without you this book would not be possible. Words may not express my heartfelt thank you, but once again thanks.

Table of Contents

Dedication
3

In Loving Memory
5

Acknowledgements
7

Introduction
11

Chapter 1
Purpose
17

Chapter 2
Wells of Living Water
33

Chapter 3
Vision Through The Eyes
45
Of Faith
45

Chapter 4
Showers of Mercy
59

Chapter 5
Trust in God
71

Chapter 6
The Love of God
79

Chapter 7
The Offence of the Cross
91

Chapter 8
The Hope of Glory
105

Chapter 9
Expect a Miracle
117

Chapter 10
How to Overcome Feelings of Inferiority
127

Chapter 11
The Dark Side of Love
137

Chapter 12
The Power of Prayer
157

Chapter 13
Blessed Hope
167

Chapter 14
The Invitation
177

Bibliography
185

Introduction

◈◈◈

How would you characterize this generation? One man said, interestingly enough and without hesitation …"hopeless!" Perhaps you agree with that assessment; and then again maybe not. But this you can't deny—much of our news today is "bad". It travels fast. We get it instantaneously in comparison to years ago when it might have taken weeks or even months.

One only has to look around at the headlines of the daily newspaper or hear the opening lines of newscasts everywhere (e.g. CBS, CNN, ABC, etc.) to discover a nation in peril. There are many people who struggle daily with depression and anxiety. The National Anxiety Center in New Jersey released the "Top Ten Fears" for the Year 2010. They are: (1) out of control government spending; (2) Iran; (3) Afghanistan war; (4) the economy; (5) inflation; (6) Medicare; (7) illegal immigration and amnesty; (8) education; (9) diet and health; and (10) American culture.

We see the economic woes of a nation in recession in addition to worldwide terrorist attacks and global warming.

A top story coming out of CNN addresses the issue of the effects of global warming. Look at the headline … "Global Warming Causing Climate Change Forces Eskimos to Abandon Their Village":

> *(CNN)—The indigenous people of Alaska have stood firm against some of the most extreme weather conditions on Earth for thousands of*

years. But now, flooding blamed on climate change is forcing at least one Eskimo village to move to safer ground. The community of the tiny coastal village of Newtok voted to relocate its 340 residents to new homes 9 miles away, up the Ninglick River. The village, home to indigenous Yup'ik Eskimos, is the first of possibly scores of threatened Alaskan communities that could be abandoned.

Scores of people around the world struggle daily with anxieties and depression: an affluent entrepreneur loses his business, then his home. Listen and you can hear the cry of troubled hearts: *"Don't talk to me about war in Afghanistan; my war-zone is my home."* Listen to the cry of a lonely heart: *"We have a nice home and a nice car. I guess you would say we're wealthy; but my husband doesn't love me anymore, and I don't know what to do!"* Some carry the scars of yesterday: *"I was raped until the age of seventeen and the emotional scars have torn my marriage apart."* Hear the cry of a slave in the "midnight trade" in the shadows of the night … *"my bishop is my predator, but my uncle turned me out Why can't anyone hear my scream?"* *"I'm tired of selling my body. Is this all there is? I feel like a piece of meat on display. Life is not worth living, but I'm so afraid of dying."* ….The cycle is vicious…the abuse so severe. Voices, cries, —rivers that seem uncross able … someone's heart is breaking even now. Listen closely…

> *The willow weeps,*
> *Underneath her branches comes a silent cry.*
> *Be still my foolish heart,*
> *Lest someone hear you break.*
>
> Wes Belfrey (2005)

Come closer, can you see the reflection of your anxiety staring back at you? Maybe not, but raise your hand if any of the following describes you.

Introduction

You get along just fine with everyone? Every relationship you have is as sweet as apple pie? You need no forgiveness? Never made a mistake of any kind, as clean as a whistle, as pure as the morning dew. Is that you? No?

Honestly speaking, let's take another look.

A few of your relationships are shaky at best. You have fears and faults. Hmmm, sounds to me as if you could use some hope for a troubled heart too.

A man who worked for a brokerage house on Wall Street wrote a few lines from his company's newsletter – lines that point out the prevailing tension of our day:

> *This is the age of the half-read page,*
> *And a quick hash and a mad dash;*
> *The bright night with the nerves tight,*
> *The plane hop and the brief stop,*
> *The lamp tan in a short span,*
> *The big shot in a soft spot,*
> *The brain strain and the heart pain.*
> *The catnaps till the spring snaps*
> *And the funs gone.*

Could this be an accurate characterization of our time? There is stress and tension everywhere and we are popping more pills than ever before. Somewhere I read that an estimated eight billion amphetamine pills are produced in our country every year. There are pills to relieve weariness; pills to put us to sleep; pills to keep awake; pills to assist in weight reduction. People used to take simple aspirin. Now there's the stronger stuff – pills that are addictive. We are hooked on pills; hooked on a feeling; hooked on a pharmaceutical drug – induced high. It's not only the drunkard on skid row, but the upper class employee of the DMV, who cozies up at home with her lover "meth." Her name has changed, heroin, pot, white lighting, crack and cocaine, but her spirit is the same. She's a scarlet whore, crouching in the dark corners of our modern world and springing forth with a new viciousness.

In her embrace are hip-hop moguls steppin, snappin, "fo shizle ma nizzle" kickin rocks; shouting it's on and poppin'; spitting venomous poison into the heart's of the innocent and naïve. But shots are fired, someone's screaming; "Oh my God! my God not me, Oh my God not me!" Her crimes are insidious and the perpetrators without remorse, as drug wars accelerate; leaving death in their wake and hell at the gate.

We as a nation have raced toward bankruptcy being more than four-trillion dollars in debt: a nation whose most powerful congressmen are indicted for criminal activities, sexual harassment, and operating homosexual dating services out of their basement; we have become a nation of drive-by shootings with a crime wave that overwhelms our judicial system; a nation where a woman is raped every forty-eight hours; a nation whose greed has caused the defense department to spend $1,200 for a coffee pot and $700 for a toilet seat. From every country in the world come stories of drug-related shootings. Yes, it's a travesty! But the saddest of all these casualties are the innocent children caught in the line of fire. I know of kids in their early teens that have the mentality of a hardened criminal.

In the city of Los Angeles alone, police officers make drug busts at a rate of over a thousand per week—and that's less than one-fourth of what they think the real story is.

Communities are being ravaged by drugs or torn apart by poverty. And teenage promiscuity is off the scale. Even the foundation of our society—the family—is being destroyed by alcoholism, infidelity or chemical addiction. The moral foundation of our country is in danger of crumbling as families breakup and parents neglect their responsibilities.

But that is not the scope of my attention in writing this book. Herein lies an invitation. Yes, an invitation extended to you. You're invited to come in and find "hope for your troubled heart."

Are you at the end of your rope? Have you lost your hope? Then my friend this book is for you. Let's begin with one of my favorite hymns.

Introduction

The Solid Rock

*My hope is built on nothing less
Than Jesus' blood and righteousness;
I dare not trust the sweetest frame,
But wholly lean on Jesus' name.
When darkness veils His lovely face,
I rest on His unchanging grace;
In ev'ry high and stormy gale
My anchor holds within the veil.*

*His oath, His covenant, His blood
Support me in the whelming flood;
When all around my soul gives way,
He then is all my hope and stay.*

*When He shall come with trumpet sound,
O may I then in Him be found,
Dressed in His righteousness alone,
Faultless to stand before the throne.*

*On Christ, the solid rock, I stand-
All other ground is sinking sand,
All other ground is sinking sand.*

Edward Mote

Chapter 1
Purpose

☙❧

*I must preach the kingdom of God...
Because for this purpose I have been sent.*

(Luke 4:43)

The man without a purpose is like a ship without a rudder — waif, a nothing, a no man. Have a purpose in life, and, having it, throw such strength of mind and muscle into your work as God has given you.

Thomas Carlyle

James Allen, British-born American essayist and author of *As a Man Thinketh*, wrote:

To put away aimlessness and weakness, and to begin to think with purpose, is to enter the ranks of those strong ones who only recognize failure as one of the pathways to attainment; who make all conditions serve them, and who think strongly, attempt fearlessly, and accomplish masterfully.

James Allen

Created With a Plan, Packed For a Purpose

We are born prepackaged at birth. God had already taken a full assessment of your entire life while you were still in your mother's womb, determined your assignment and equipped you with the tools to do the job. Recently my wife and I took a trip to Washington, D. C. But before traveling we did something similar. We considered the purpose of our trip—a family reunion. And so we packed accordingly. If it's hot weather, bring a straw hat, short sleeves, and light clothing and don't forget the sunglasses. On the other hand, if it's a football game, bring binoculars and popcorn money. Should it be a day with the grandchildren: better bring patience!

Did not God do the same with us? Nathan will be an architect and Mechille, an accountant: give them a fascination with mathematics; Martha will be a principal: an extra dose of education and managerial skills; I need Chris to comfort the sick: instill a healthy share of compassion; Ruth will marry Billy: infuse a double portion of patience. God packed you on purpose for His divine purpose!

The Sanctity of the Home

The most important group of people mentioned in the Bible is the family. The Old Testament Hebrew word meeshpacha (mish-paw-khaw') when translated means "tribe". The New Testament counterpart patria (pä-trē-ä') means "lineage".

The family unit is so important that the first chapter of Matthew lists all the generations in the lineage of Jesus. Today's families would translate this into family reunions where all the relatives and in-laws connected by marriage are included as part of a family.

The primary role of a family in the Bible was to build strong relationships with each other. It was substantiated by the way members treated those within the family unit, as well as their neighbors and the strangers they met. Within the family there should be protection and nurturing. Apostle Paul tells about the family being the place where spiritual nurturing is to begin (1 Timothy 5:4). As parents we have

Purpose

the responsibility of showing our children the importance of a godly home.

We are a far cry from Bible days. The traditional family is now represented by one in four families—yes, one in four families live together as the traditional mother and father with their children.

English Historian Edward Gibbon wrote the masterpiece, *The Decline and Fall of the Roman Empire*. He gives six reasons for the collapse of the Roman Empire:

First, he cites the rapid increase of divorce; secondly, was the ridicule of the sanctity of the home; thirdly, were escalating taxes with a waste of public funds; fourthly, was a mad craze for pleasure which became increasingly exciting and at the same time, more brutal; fifthly, speaking of the Roman coliseums, there were the enormous armaments for war while the nation decayed internally; and lastly, was the decline of faith in God, which became a mere form.

Perilous Times

We see the devastating results of family failure all around us—child abuse, teenage pregnancy, abortions, suicides and runaways. There are conflicts of every sort—religious, cultural and political—wars and rumors of wars just as racism seeks the annihilation of the very fabric of our lives.

If the foundations be destroyed what can the righteous do? America was built on a covenant relationship with God. If you read The Mayflower Compact, it is pure and simply … a covenant with God. America was founded by men who honored God and set their founding principles by the words of the Bible. They lived their lives with honesty, integrity, dependability, and justice toward establishing this country "for the sake of its survival". A great many of America's founding fathers have been quoted in regard to living by biblical values.

Patrick Henry (1736-1799), five-term governor of Virginia, whose *Give Me Liberty or Give Me Death* speech has made him immortal, said:

Hope For A Troubled Heart

It cannot be emphasized too strongly or too often that this great nation was founded, not by religionists, but by Christians, not on religions, but on the gospel of Jesus Christ!

We've seen national disasters on a horrific scale. The 2004 Indian Ocean earthquake was an undersea earthquake that occurred on December 26, 2004, with an epic centre off the west coast of Sumatra, Indonesia. It was a catastrophic earthquake that triggered a series of devastating tsunamis along the coast of most landmasses bordering the Indian Ocean which resulted in the deaths of more than 225,000 people, and dispaced people in fourteen countries while inundating coastal communities with waves up to 100 feet high. Among natural disasters, it is known as one of the deadliest in recorded history.

It would seem as though our world is in a tailspin—from piracy on the high seas, rumors of genocide in Sudan, to the furious outrage against Israel by Mahmoud Ahmadinejad (leader of Iran). Nation is against nation and kingdom against kingdom.

One of the sad realities of our day is that military spending is bankrupting the nations of the world. It brought down the Soviet Union, and it is the reason for the huge deficit in our country. Meanwhile, there are people all over the world who are starving to death, even though there is enough food in the world to feed everyone. Imagine if we could take all the resources that are presently invested in defense spending and focus all that effort and all those resources on feeding the poor. World hunger would come to an end immediately. And that is exactly what will happen when Jesus rules and there is no more need for a military buildup.

The prophet Micah speaks of the day when weapons will be turned into farming instruments. *"Swords will be turned into plowshares and spears into pruning hooks; nation shall not lift up sword against nation, neither shall they learn war any more"* (Mic. 4:3). This scripture has been an inspiration to

Purpose

many of us for so many years. Many politicians have latched onto this prediction of peace which is carved into the corner stone of the United Nations building. They have suggested that this could be brought about through good government. But this peace won't come to pass until Jesus, the Prince of Peace, returns to rule and reign on this earth.

But Satan has launched a gigantic propaganda campaign against the stream of Christian thought which is designed to separate us from the prophetic truth of scripture. One way in which he does this is by polluting our minds with programs on television and other outlets that are filled with lewdness, debauchery, sex and violence. Inevitably what appears as an intense storm suddenly transforms into a blazing inferno.

However, if I were to focus on these things alone, it would be easy to lose hope. But that must not be the focal point of our attention. We have a hope. It is an everlasting, unshakable hope. It is a hope founded upon truth. It is the hope of salvation that we have in a relationship with God through his Son Jesus Christ. And when I'm troubled, when I'm dismayed, I turn to Him. I run to Him in prayer. He speaks peace to my troubled heart and calms the raging sea within my soul. Francis Schaeffer said, *"God is there, and He's not silent. He speaks and we can hear Him, if we listen."* I've had experiences in my life when I needed God desperately; He was always there.

It was late one night during the summer of 1971, in Compton, California, a suburb of Los Angeles. I was walking home from a revival that evening, singing and rejoicing unto the Lord: *"Amazing grace how sweet the sound that saved a wretch like me."* Reports of violence and gang activity seemed to dominate the news. But I had no choice in the matter. I had to walk home. I had no transportation of my own, and to make matters worse I didn't even have bus fare. I noticed a group of young men from across the street. They were just hanging out. At least I thought that was the case. So minding my own business, I kept stepping.

Suddenly, I heard footsteps running from behind; "Was I they're next victim? Were they coming for me?" As I stopped and turned, a short little fellow, about my height was the first to approach. Looking down at my bible in hand, he sneered saying, "Oh you a church boy huh—you a church boy!" What should I do, what should I say? I responded with a smile, and without reservation I reached into my bible handing each one a tract which said; "are you working for wages? The wages of sin is death. Or would you rather have a free gift? The gift of God is eternal life through Jesus Christ our Lord." By now I was anointed to share the gospel; "Yes brother, I just got out of church and what a time we had in the Lord!"

By this time I was surrounded with no place of retreat. However, much to my amazement I remained calm as I continued on to say, "Brothers can you walk with me down the road a bit. I'd like to give you my testimony of how Jesus saved me from sin."

After a brief pause, as if bewildered, the gang leader said, "Ok man, we'll listen." That's all I needed to hear. My "preacher" kicked in and boy did I preach. I spoke of my hope of salvation in Christ Jesus as we walked along the road, answering their questions as best I could.

As we talked this one brother who was smashed came over, pushed me in the chest. He reeked with alcohol. That wasn't so bad but there was something in his eyes—something menacing; something diabolical. Was it murder? I really didn't know, but his words were on fire—hell fire. I did not respond. And as we stood there face-to-face, eyeball-to-eyeball, no more words were exchanged, only an ominous silence.

Was it about to go down? Was I the lamb before the lion? Or was I the prey before the predator? The pack froze and so did I. And I thought, "What now?"

But the Lord was my stay. He had my back, and this one guy stepped up, pushed him aside and demanded that he shut up and let me talk.

Purpose

So I continued on, full speed ahead, sharing Jesus and how His love lifted me, "Jesus can save you, my brothers, He can do for you, what He did for me." I was high in the Holy Ghost and His grace was truly amazing. My only regret is that I didn't extend an invitation to each one to accept Christ. Finally as we parted, I invited them all to the revival; what was intended for evil, the Lord turned out for good—theirs and mines. His compassions they fail not. His faithfulness is great indeed. We have access to everything God has promised to His people in His Holy Word. And because I know that God loves me and my life is in His hands, I have hope for tomorrow.

In every circumstance, in every situation, I'm God's workmanship created in Christ Jesus unto good works according to the power that works within me. He is the God of all power and He desires to empower you with supernatural strength for the task at hand. He is the God of all hope, the anchor of my soul and He gives us a solid foundation upon which we stand and base our hope.

We were made for a purpose. We were made in the image of God after His likeness. You are exceptional and what makes you that way is your uniqueness. Not only is there a physical characteristic that celebrates your individuality, but each of us has a unique heartbeat as well. Each heart beats in a slightly different rhythmic pattern; no one has a heartbeat quite like yours. Additionally, no one else has the same DNA as you. And yes, we were created to live a meaningful life. Why do you suppose so many people resort to counterfeit solutions like astrology or psychics in search of the true meaning of life? And we know that the Bible repeatedly warns us against having anything to do with these, but people are trying to discover the true meaning to life. When your life has meaning you can bear just about anything. Maybe you say, "Wes I feel like a failure, because I'm struggling to become something that I don't even know what it really is. All I know is how to get by."

My friend, life without God has no meaning, and without purpose life has no hope.

Knowing His purpose, the Apostle Paul sang and shouted his way through his trials. His greatest victories came out of his persecutions. To the Romans, he wrote:

> ...*We also rejoice in our sufferings, because we know that suffering produces perseverance, and perseverance, character; and character, hope. And hope does not disappoint us, because God has poured out His love into our hearts by the Holy Ghost, whom He has given us*

(Romans 5:3-5)

Have you ever wondered about your purpose in life? Why were you created? Have you ever asked the question, Why am I here? We all have asked "why" at one time or another. It maybe the frustrations of life—perhaps the nagging despair you can't seem to shake. Sometimes it's the dreaded fear of growing old alone and unwanted. Not to mention the relentless worries that follow you home to steal your sleep in the night or the anxieties of living paycheck to paycheck. Sometimes we're blindsided by sudden winds of adversity and hardship striking a blow, cutting us down, and leaving us stunned as our knees buckle sending our barometers plummeting to the bottom of the gauge.

David asked, "Why?" "*Why are you cast down, O my soul?*" (Psalms 42:5) In other words, why are you depressed? "*And why are you disquieted within me?*" In today's vernacular we might say, "Why am I so depressed? Why am I filled with such anxiety?" We feel trapped; we feel under pressure; we are overwhelmed; we are tired of being tired, and sick of being sick; we can't see a way out. But David didn't stop there. He went on to say, "*Hope in God!*" (Psalms 42:5) The reason we become depressed and cast down is that I've lost sight of God. He has been removed from the equation. I am trying to figure out a solution without faith in Him. The answer is to put God back in the equation. Then that which is impossible becomes possible because all things are possible with God.

Several years ago, there was a weekly television show called Quantum Leap. In this series, the young fellow would jump in and out of various time zones.

If there ever was a "quantum leap", this is it … finite man could live in communion with an infinite God! The One who existed long before the universe was created and the One who transcends time and space, has chosen to become one with man in communion, sharing in fellowship.

This becomes truly awesome when you realize how great and immeasurable our God is. He fills the entire universe and yet He desires fellowship with us. When I think about this, it is incomprehensible!

But as we study the Bible we come to understand that this is the very purpose of our existence. We exist for the purpose of having fellowship and intimacy with God. "… *That which we have seen and heard we declare to you, that you also may have fellowship with us; and truly our fellowship is with the Father and with His Son Jesus Christ*" (1 Jn. 1:3). The fact that I can have fellowship with God is phenomenal!

The very nature of hope requires that we have some sense of meaning and purpose to our lives. The Word of God says that you have a purpose and you are loved more than you know. God has a plan for your life and it's a wonderful plan. In Jeremiah, God says "*For I know the plans I have for you,*" declares the Lord, "*plans to prosper you and not to harm you, plans to give you hope and a future.*" (Jeremiah 29:11) In essence He's saying, "I'm concerned with your peace, and I'm concerned with the end result."

God never thinks of you in terms of evil, but always in terms of what's best for you. As far as God is concerned, the most important thing for you is that you spend eternity with Him. We are always preoccupied with our present comfort and happiness. When I'm in a situation that makes me uncomfortable, I may say, "I don't like this! Has God forsaken me?" But many times we complain about those very things that God is using to shape and prepare us for eternity.

Abraham's Faith in Purpose
Abraham knew his purpose and by faith he received the promise of God to become the father of a multitude. God said, "*I have made you a father of many nations*" (Gen. 17:5b). The Apostle Paul speaks concerning Abraham's faith saying that his body was dead (impotent) and Sarah was also past the age of childbearing (Romans 4). God did not want Abraham trying to fulfill the promise in his own strength. So He allowed him to come to the place in his life where it was impossible for him to fulfill the promise himself. It would take a miracle. God often as He works His plan for our lives will allow us to come to the end of ourselves and our resources. And lets us come to that place of hopelessness before He works so that He is glorified when He fulfills His promise to us.

Abraham believed the promise of God that he would have a son at the age of one hundred and against hope he believed in hope being strong in faith that he might become the father of many nations. And even though the situation seemed hopeless, his body being dead in relation to childbearing, he staggered not at the promise of God through unbelief.

The Jews to this very day look back to Abraham as their father. So Paul used Abraham as an example of righteousness. He turned back to Genesis when God instituted His covenant with Abraham. The testimony of the scriptures was that "*Abraham believed God, and He accounted it to him for righteousness*"(Genesis 15:5-7). This truth will never change. Abraham could not be justified by his works, and therefore he had nothing to boast about. And so it is with us today just as it was with Abraham, we are only justified by faith in God.

It's incredible how God not only forgives us of all sin, but also clears the soul from the guilt of sin, placing us in His sight cleansed from all unrighteousness. He wipes the slate clean and there's no charge to your account. The debt of sin

Purpose

has been paid in full—that's justification!

> *The eternal God is thy refuge,*
> *and underneath are the everlasting arms...*
>
> *(Deuteronomy 33:27)*

In his letter to the Philippians, Paul gives relevant and wise counsel to those of us who worry and are filled with anxiety. He says:

> *Rejoice in the Lord always; again I will say, rejoice! Let your gentleness be known to all men. The Lord is at hand. Be anxious for nothing, but in everything by prayer and supplication with thanksgiving, let your requests be made known to God. And the peace of God, which surpasses all understanding, will guard your hearts and minds through Christ Jesus*
>
> *(Philippians 4:4-7)*

We are part of a generation where people are desperately searching for the purpose of life. The fact of the matter is if you don't know why you are here, it leaves you with a feeling of emptiness inside or with a sense of hopelessness, without direction and meaning to your life, meandering aimlessly upon a restless sea of existence.

All of us are searching for meaning and fulfillment and we live under the illusion that if I had more money, I would be happy. If I could just win the lottery, hit the jackpot, swing from the chandelier one more night. But true happiness can never come from the glories of this world.

Yet, because of its promises, we have a tendency to gravitate toward the world in hopes of finding fulfillment. We go from one pursuit to another, one escapade to another, from casino to race track, one affair to another. Then comes the emptiest moment of your life when you have achieved and attained all the success you hoped would bring you fulfillment, only to realize you are still empty. The dream is not the same, the glory gone with the winds of change, and the party is over.

The Bible is very clear as to what man's purpose should be. Solomon, the wisest man who ever lived, discovered the futility of life when it is lived only for the glories of this world. He sums up these conclusions in the book of Ecclesiastes, *"Here is the conclusion of the matter: Fear God and keep His commandment, for this is the whole duty of man. For God will bring every deed into judgment, including every hidden thing, whether it is good or evil"* (Eccl. 12:13-14). Solomon says that life is all about honoring God with our lives and therefore keeping His commandments. For one day we will stand before Him in judgment. So it is part of our purpose in life to have a reverential respect for God (which is called the fear of the Lord) and to honor and obey Him.

The first four commandments which constitute the first tablet of the Law, address your relationship with God. The other six address your relationships with your fellowman, how I relate to others. If you'd violated one of the first four commandments, you were considered to be ungodly since these commandments related to the Lord God. However, if you were to violate the second thru the sixth commandment, then you were considered to be unrighteous. Therefore, if a person is first ungodly, then it stands to reason he will be unrighteous as well. So your relationship with God is key and it determines how well you relate to those around you. We cannot even hope to keep the next six commandments unless we keep the first four. Unless my relationship with God is right, my relationship with man cannot be right. Often when people have relationship problems, whether it's with their marriage, parents, or children, they try to solve the problem without first examining their own personal relationship with God. This would be treating the symptom versus the problem.

Purpose

Secondly, we are to see life here on earth in proper biblical perspective. David looked for his satisfaction in the future. He said, "*And I—in righteousness I will see your face; when I awake, I will be satisfied with seeing your likeness*" (Ps. 17:15). David would not be satisfied until the day when he awoke (in the resurrection), both beholding the face of Jesus Christ and being like Him. The Apostle Paul talked about all he had achieved as a religious man before being confronted by the risen Christ, and he concluded that all of it was like a hill of manure compared to the excellence of knowing Christ Jesus. He affirms his position in Philippians by saying that he wants nothing more than to know Christ and "*be found in Him*" (Philippians 3:9), having His righteousness and to live by faith in Him, even if it meant suffering and dying.

The Apostle's purpose was to know Christ, having a righteousness obtained through faith in Him, and living in fellowship with Him, even when it entailed suffering (2 Timothy 3:12). And ultimately, he looked forward to the time when he would be a part of the "resurrection from the dead."

Our purpose in life is first to glorify God and enjoy fellowship with Him: secondly, to love one another. Jesus said, "*A new commandment I give to you, that you love one another; as I have loved you, that you also love one another*" (Jn. 13:34). God is generous in His love. He is also pleased when we express His love to others as well and when we receive it in return.

I believe the word to describe the nature of God more than any other word is love. The very essence of God's being is love. The purpose for God sending Jesus into this world was love. "*For God so loved the world that He gave His only begotten Son that whosoever believeth in Him should not perish but have everlasting life*" (Jn. 3:16). In 1 John, we are told that the attribute of God is love. John based this conclusion on his personal relationship with Jesus—having walked with Him for nearly three years of ministry before His crucifixion and resurrection.) It's several decades after Jesus ascended back to glory to be with the Father, that he records his testimony:

> "We have seen and do testify that the Father has sent the Son as Savior of the world. Whoever confesses that Jesus is the Son of God, God abides in him, and he in God. And we have known and believed the love that God has for us. God is love, and he who abides in love abides in God, and God in him."

(1 John 4:14-16)

But how do I respond to a love like that? The Bible teaches us that we should respond with our hearts. I accept Christ by faith into my heart. Jesus said: to "love the Lord thy God with all thy heart."

Throughout the Bible the word "heart" is used to describe the many desires, hopes, aspirations, dreams, and affections a person has. It is your heart that represents the true source of all your motivations such as your enjoyments—the walks in the cool of the day with that someone special when time stood still and you felt love's chill underneath a quarter moon. Even today, we find ourselves using the word "heart" when we say, "I've fallen in love with you, and I love you with all of my heart."

The Bible urges us to, "*Keep your heart with all diligence, for out of it springs the issues of life*" (Proverbs 4:21). Open your heart and you reveal who you are—I mean the real you, not the façade you project for all to see. Your words are expressions of your heart, and they are influenced by what's in your heart. Why is it that you feel the way you do? And why do you act the way you do? I'll tell you why ... it's what's in your heart. Sometimes when we express our heart's desire we may use the word "passion". What drives you? What's the conviction of your heart? There are some subjects we feel very passionate about, while others simply bore us.

Purpose

As a young teenage boy I became fascinated by something that no one else in my family really cared about at all. I remember it like it was yesterday. It was the house on Gage Avenue—right off the freeway. We were settling in our new home. I noticed the previous occupants had left behind an old stereo system and I was a curious teenager when I came across an album which said, At Last by Nat King Cole. As I listened to the title song I was hooked! It was something about Nate's voice that was soothing. And I wanted to be smooth like Nate. So I learned each song on that album—practicing hours on end. When my brothers were outside playing, I'd be in my room singing a song. My passion in life, my heart's desire was to sing his songs. Flibby and Faye, my elder sisters, would laugh and say, "Boy, you sound like an old frog." But Dad would smile and say, "That's alright, keep practicing; practice makes perfect." That's all I needed to hear. I loved my dad, and what he did that day validated, or confirmed my passion for my music. My life was consumed with it. I was a man on fire.

Then late one night while on my way home from the Los Angeles Skating Rink, thinking about my dream of success, my name in lights, how it's going to be when I'm rich and famous, God interrupted my trend of thought. And He did so with a question. It was not an audible voice, but I heard Him just as clear as a bell, "What if you make it to the top of the ladder of success? What shall it profit a man if he shall gain this whole world and lose his own soul, or what shall a man give in exchange for his soul." Looking up towards heaven I thought about eternity, while my dream seemed to fade and crumble before me. That was the turning point in my life and shortly thereafter I went to a prayer meeting in my mother's home, fell on my knees and accepted Christ. Yes, at last my dream had come true. No not through fortune, fame and riches in Hollywood, but in the riches of glory in Christ Jesus.

Chapter 2
Wells of Living Water

꧁꧂

Water is the most abundant liquid on the planet, covering approximately 70 percent of the earth's surface. We as humans are composed mostly of water—our bodies are 55 percent to 75 percent water. Pure water is tasteless, odorless and colorless. However it does have a blue shade in large volumes. The familiar chemical symbol H20 means that water molecules are composed of 2 hydrogen atoms and 1 oxygen atom. Our blood contains 95 percent water and our body fat contains 14 percent water.

The first mention of water in the Bible is found in Genesis 1:2 and the last mention is found in Revelation 22:17. And in between these two books, water flows like a mighty river throughout the entire scripture.

Water in the scripture is a symbol of the Holy Ghost, which God promised to pour out upon His Church. It symbolizes life. Jesus said, *"Come. And let him that is athirst come"* (Rev. 22:17).

We all have a thirst deep down inside, a spiritual thirst that can only be satisfied by a relationship with God. David penned, *"As the deer pants for the water brooks, so pants my soul for You, O God. My soul thirsts for God, for the living God"* (Psalms 42:1-2). We all have a huge spiritual need that can only be filled by God. We know we are thirsty, but we try to satisfy that thirst with physical things or with emotional experiences. But all of these things offer only temporary relief, and the excitement of our new toys eventually gives way to that nagging thirst again. So we pursue an endless quest of unsatisfying acquisitions supposing that we will experience satisfaction eventually. Or we give up on ultimate satisfaction and settle for temporary relief that comes in spurts. But Jesus announced that He is the One who can satisfy the thirst that is in the heart of everyone. And He will do it by overflowing our hearts with the Spirit. He alone can fill the emptiness inside. For the one who comes to Him, He promises that out of your life will spring forth torrents of living water. This He spoke concerning the Holy Spirit.

The "New Birth" Experience

We know what being born of the Spirit is. It is the new birth--being born of God. When we receive Christ, we receive His Spirit into our hearts and we are born again of His Spirit. *"As many as received Him to them He gave power to become the sons of God, even to them that believe on His name: which were born not of blood, nor of the will of the flesh, nor of the will of man, but of God"* (Jn. 1:12-13).

The Holy Spirit

Some say the Spirit is a reward for commitment. This belief, however may limit my faith. If I believe I can't receive the baptism of the Spirit until I have made some level of commitment, then I am not apt to accept this gift of God by faith, not until I have felt that I have attained that degree of commitment. And so my belief system can hinder my faith from simply trusting God to fill me. If I set certain criteria for my faith outside the bounds of scripture, which is the foundation for my faith, then I may limit my faith, hindering what God wants to do in my life. In Galatians, Apostle Paul asked the question," *Did you receive the Holy Ghost by the works of the Law or by the hearing of faith?"* (Galatians 3:2)

There are some people who even tell you that it is dangerous to ask for the Holy Spirit. They say that you open yourself up to all sorts of dangerous phenomena if you ask God to fill you with His Spirit. That is not only wrong, but that's blasphemous. As we have need for spiritual nourishment and as we recognize the need we have for the Holy Spirit to fill our hearts and empower our lives, we can be assured that our loving heavenly Father will respond to that prayer by guarding us from the evil one and filling us with His Spirit.

In Luke Jesus says, "If you then, being evil, (natural), know how to give good gifts to your children, how much more will your heavenly Father give The Holy Spirit to those who ask Him!" (Luke 11:13) An earthly father wouldn't give your son a scorpion when he asks for an egg. In other words, if a son asks his father for food, his father won't respond by giving something that will harm him. How much more likely that your heavenly Father would never give you something harmful when you are asking for something that is as necessity as The Holy Spirit! What did Jesus say? *"Ask and it will be given to you..."* (Matt. 7:7).

Jesus said that He would send the Holy Ghost to those who believe. And He is the One who seals the presence of Christ in our hearts. So the question my friend is simply this—do you believe?

Jesus said when the Holy Ghost has come upon you, you will receive power to live in such a way that you will become a reflection of Him. That's what being a witness is really all about—your life becomes a witness. Someone once asked the question, "If you were arrested for being a Christian, would there be enough evidence to convict you?"

My wife Delores is an amazing woman of God. She was saved at the young age of fifteen. One day while sitting meditating on the Lord, she recalls a sudden feeling of great thirst. So in simple childlike prayer she asked God, "O Lord, quench my thirst and fill this emptiness." And immediately God answered, and filled her with His Spirit. In Matthew Jesus said, *"Blessed are those who hunger and thirst for righteousness for they shall be filled..."* (Matthew 5:6).

A good illustration of this comes to us from Greek mythology in a picture of a mighty man holding a great urn upon his shoulder. Out of this urn he's pouring forth a mighty stream both from the East and to the West and finally flowing into the mouth or over the body of a fish. He is the One who pours out the water upon Piscis-Australis, the Southern fish.

Just as fish need water to survive, the believer needs the Spirit of God for survival. He is the well-spring of the believer's life. It is then imperative that believers strive after this life.

Years ago there was a popular hit song entitled "Aquarius." But what does Aquarius mean? The real meaning has nothing to do with Astrology, which is satanic. And again the Bible repeatedly warns us against having anything to do with this perversion of the truth. "Aquarius" comes from the root meanings of "the water" and "bearer", when translated means "the pourer forth of water".

It is Christ, Who is the "water-bearer," pouring out the water of the Holy Ghost upon His Church, the living fish. All throughout the Bible we see the continuity of God pouring His Spirit like water upon a thirsty land and all who are athirst can come and drink. *"And the Spirit and the bride say come…and let him that is athirst come and whosoever will, let him take the water of life freely"* (Rev. 22:17).

Shadow of a great Rock In a weary land

When the children of Israel were traveling through the wilderness, they pitched in Rephidim; and there was no water for the people to drink. They complained against Moses, and said; give us water to drink. Why have you brought us out of Egypt to die of thirst in this wilderness? Isn't it funny how quickly we forget what God has done. How quickly we seem to despair. Moses cried to the lord, *"What am I to do with these people? They are almost ready to stone me. the Lord instructed him to go before the people with some of the elders so that they could witness the miracle of God. Take the rod, strike the rock, water will come out.* (Exodus 17:4-6)

Now in the New Testament, Paul the apostle tells us that rock that was with them in the wilderness was Jesus: *"That rock was Christ*" (1 Cor. 10:4). The rock smitten brought forth water of life to the people. So we have a beautiful figure of Jesus smitten on the cross to bring forth life to us. Now in New Testament we are told that these things are all figures. During the celebration of the feast of tabernacles they were celebrating how God preserved their fathers during their forty years of wondering in the wilderness. And part of the preservation was the providing of the water out of the rock. During the feast the priest would go down to the pool of Siloam with these large water jugs, and fill them with water. Then, they would come back up to the steps where several hundred thousand Jews were gathered in the great temple mount area, and in front of all of the people; the priest would pour the water out on the pavement of the temple mount saying: "*Therefore with joy shall you draw water out of the wells of salvation.*" (Isaiah 12:3) This was to remind them of how God gave their fathers water out of the rock there in the wilderness.

Now Jesus, the Fountain of living waters; stood on the last day of the feast and cried: "*If anyone thirsts, let him come to Me and drink. He who believes in Me as the Scripture has said, out of his heart will flow rivers of living water.*" (John 7:38)

In Genesis, we read of the first mention of life, and this life comes from water, "...Let the waters bring forth abundantly the living creatures..." (Genesis 1:20). Now concerning spiritual life, when Nicodemus, a ruler of the Jews, asked in John concerning spiritual birth, Jesus responded, "*Except a man be born of water and of the Spirit, he cannot enter into the kingdom of God.*" (John 3:5) Notice how the water birth (physical) comes before the Spirit birth (spiritual).

When Delores was in labor with each of our children, we were told to wait for the 'water bag to break' which surrounded the baby until birth. We cannot be spiritually reborn until we have first been naturally born.

Hope For A Troubled Heart

*"He makes me lie down in green pastures,
He leads me beside the still waters."*

(Psalms 23:2)

The average American is exposed to more than three hundred advertisements a day. They're all over the place—billboards, magazines, shiny bright colors, slick ads, appealing print and pictures—designed to hijack your concentration and steal your attention. Before you realize it, you're hoodwinked and bamboozled by the Madison Avenue Pied Piper who has led you into a world of exaggerated make-believe in which you are convinced that you simply can't live without it—a new DVD player, Blu-ray with HDTV, a set of his and hers Rolex watches, a brand new Lincoln Navigator to park in front of your new house on a hill. And the many other television, full-color missiles that explode in your imagination with the messages, "Try me, you'll see. You deserve the very best."

Such commercialism does a real number on us. Some of the results are obvious. They stimulate our curiosity. They urge us to buy goods or services. They make us aware of what is available while they announce new merchandise, shaping our tastes, habits, and customs. It's "the American way" and intricately interwoven into our economy of capitalism. After all, it's a multi-billion dollar a year business.

But there is a subliminal message that detonates deep down inside our heads—silently yet vehemently. But if we're not careful, thoughts are embedded in the brain, conveying a damaging message.

In a word, it is discontentment ... dissatisfaction. It creates a restless drive for more, or better, or bigger. Three hundred times a day, it chips away at the damn that supports one of the last reservoirs of inner peace known to man—contentment. Full of tranquility—what a beautiful scene is the "still waters" of Contentment!

Undisturbed by outside noises brought on by the distracting jackhammers of exploitation and exaggeration, those who enjoy sitting by the still waters of the lake come to know what restful peace is all about. They know nothing of the troubling waters of discontentment. They abide under the shadow of the Almighty and dwell in His secret place. Apostle Paul lived on this lake. Remember he's the one who wrote, "*And if we have food and covering, with these we shall be content*" (1 Tim. 6:8).

Isn't it funny how easy and often we fail to apply this instruction. We find ourselves competing, grabbing, hording, seldom releasing or giving all in the name of "saving". John D. Rockefeller was once asked, "*How much does it take to satisfy a man?*" He answered, "*A little bit more than he has.*"

But does contentment mean I need to sell everything I have and never buy anything new? Does it mean I cannot have nice things? No of course not. It means those nice things don't have you. But remember becoming content is a process, never an instant reality. Earlier in his life the Apostle Paul declared, "*I have learned to be content in whatever circumstances I am. I know how to get along with humble means, and I also know how to live in prosperity. In any and every circumstance, I have learned the secret of being filled and going hungry, both of having abundance and suffering need*" (Phil. 4:11,12).

Look at the extremes of his life ... humble means, prosperity, filled, hungry, having abundance, suffering need. On the yo-yo of life, he had learned to slow down and enjoy whatever circumstances came his way. And then when his circumstances improved, the apostle had no anxiety in encountering "the good life". He equally enjoyed hot dogs as well as a filet mignon, a vacation on the "Riviera" or under the bridge. How? His focus was right on target. He held every earthly thing loosely. He refused to leave the still waters of "lake contentment" in search of some shallow stream that was sure to dry up. He knew the joy of drawing from the well that never shall run dry. You can do that too. But it will take the grace of God and all the discipline you can muster up, "casting all your care upon Him, for He cares for you."

Water Speaks To Us of the Word of God

Apostle Paul in Ephesians, addresses one aspect of the Church in relation to the word of God ... *"That He might sanctify and cleanse it with the washing of water by the word"* (Ephesians 5:26). The Psalmist writes, *"How can a young man cleanse his way? By taking heed according to Your word"* (Psalm 119:9) Reading the Bible has a cleansing effect on us. In Exodus Moses was to make a laver of brass and put water in it. It was to be placed between the tabernacle and the altar. The priests were to wash their hands and feet in it when they went into the tabernacle "that they die not." They needed to be purified. (Exodus 30:18)

But to us now there is a fountain open for Judah and Jerusalem to wash in (Zechariah 13:1). The song writer says ... *"Sinners plunge beneath the flood and lose all their guilt and stain."* This is an inexhaustible fountain of living water that cleanses from all unrighteousness. We see a New Testament picture of this in John, where Jesus is washing the disciples' feet. Peter soon realizes the importance of this cleansing: *"Lord, not my feet only, but also my hands and my head."* Jesus said to him, *"He that is washed needs not save to wash his feet, but is clean every whit: and you are clean, but not all"* (John 13:5-14).

John records this ceremony that Christ performed and instituted on the night of His betrayal. It may at first seem strange that the other three synoptic gospel writers did not address this act at all. But if you look a little closer, it makes perfect sense why God chose John to record it. The foot washing ceremony is at its root an act of love. So, who is better to give account of this than *"the disciple whom Jesus loved"* (John 21:7).

Washing one another's feet is also an act of humility when we perform it as Christ instructs us. While it indeed should be done with a humble attitude, there is also a deeper and more meaningful explanation why it is so vital that we do it with a good understanding. This will help us to realize how important Christ's example is to us today. Then again,

John probably recognized the direct connection between foot washing and the awesome work of the Savior in His life, death, and resurrection.

We are defiled within and without. Inwardly, we are defiled by the power and pollution of sin and in our carnal nature. Apostle Paul in Romans, described the struggle that is within every person who is trying to lead a good life. We want to do the right thing and we are determined to do the right thing. We want to stop doing those things that are wrong. But there is a battle going on inside, and we often end up doing that which we hate and neglecting the good things we really want to do. It makes us feel wretched! We can't fix it on our own. We are unable to reform ourselves. The Apostle exclaims … *"Oh wretched man that I am! Who shall deliver me from the body of this death?"* (Romans 7:14-25)

We need outside help. For our cleansing from this we need spiritual water— water that can reach the depths of the soul. There is a fountain in Christ Jesus for the washing of regeneration and the renewing of the Holy Ghost.

At the death of Christ on the Cross, His side was pierced with a soldier's spear, and out of the wound came, like a healing stream, water and blood. John was a witness and I'm sure he was greatly affected by the sight. He alone records it and seems to consider himself grateful to record it as containing something mysterious or perhaps even miraculous. *"And he that saw it bore record, and his record is true. And he knows, being an eye-witness, that he saith true, that you might believe, and that you might believe this particularly … that out of His pierced side forthwith there came water and blood"* (John 19:34-35) Now this water and blood are inclusive of all that is necessary and efficient to our salvation. With the "washing of water by the word," our souls are washed and purified for heaven. And so *"Therefore, brethren, having boldness to enter the Holiest by the blood of Jesus, by a new and living way which He consecrated for us, through the veil, that is His flesh, and having a High Priest over the house of God, let us draw near with a true heart in full assurance of faith, having our hearts sprinkled from an evil conscience and our bodies washed with pure water"* (Heb. 10:19-22).

The other three gospel writers focus on the bread and wine that the Lord instituted that same night, making no mention of foot washing. John does just the opposite. John being the last of the gospel writers fills in some of the things Jesus and did and said that the others left out of their gospels. John no doubt felt that the foot washing ceremony needed to be included in the New Testament canon. It also allows us a window into the character of our Savior.

Immediately upon reading the account, we notice that Christ performs a basic task generally done by the lowliest servant in the household. Look at what He says in John, *"You call Me teacher and Lord, and you say well, for so I am. If I then, your Lord and Teacher, have washed your feet; you also ought to wash one another's feet. For I have given you an example, that you should do as I have done to you. Most assuredly, I say to you, a servant is not greater than his master; nor is he who is sent greater than he who sent him"* (John 13:13-16). The power of the universe is vested in Jesus. He said in Matthew, *"All authority has been given to Me in heaven and on earth"* (Mathew 28:18) John says that Jesus knew that *"the Father had given all things into His hands"* (John 13:3). What does one do with that kind of power? Jesus, on the basis of that power, girded Himself, took a towel, and washed the feet of His disciples. He used His power to serve. It has been said that "power tends to corrupt, and that absolute power corrupts absolutely." This may be true for most people, but not for the One who truly has absolute power. As Christians, we all need to be purified from the filth of this world, we all need our feet cleaned.

The "Baptism of the Holy Spirit"
Why is it that we sing, *"Fill my cup Lord, fill it up Lord, come and quench this thirsting of my soul,"* Fill me to overflowing. As cups, we are leaky vessels and each day we should seek to be filled with His Spirit. The Bible says, *"Be ye filled with*

the Spirit"(Ephesians 5:18). The present tense usage of the Greek verb "be" translates this scripture as *"Be ye continually getting filled with the Spirit of God."* We need to be continually getting filled with God's precious gift of the Holy Ghost. Let us remember the words our Lord Jesus, *"Blessed are they that hunger and thirst after righteousness, for they shall be filled"* (Mathew 5:6)

God desires that our lives be a reflection of His Son Jesus, but we can't do this by our own power. We can't forgive, and we cannot love. We don't have His compassion, or His tender care. But by the transforming power of the Holy Spirit, we can be changed into His image and be witnesses to Him.

If you have not experienced this overflowing, and if you are trying to fill your needs with other things, come to Jesus. He is the only One who can satisfy the deepest longings of your heart. He is the One who truly satisfies. In Isaiah scripture states, *"Therefore with joy you will draw water from the wells of salvation"* (Isaiah 12:3) Jesus stood up on the last day of the Feast of Tabernacles and announced, *"If anyone thirsts, let him come to Me and drink. He who believes in me as the Scripture has said, out of his heart shall flow rivers of living water"* (Jn. 7:37-38). John went on to explain that Jesus was talking about the Spirit of God (Jn. 7:39). So we see joy as a fruit of the Spirit that flows forth from the one who comes to Jesus and drinks of His living water. He told the woman at the well, *"Whoever drinks of the water that I shall give him will never thirst"* (John 4:14).

In John, as Jesus breathed on His disciples, He said to them, *"Receive the Holy Ghost."* (John 20:22) They were receiving as a believer the second part of the three-fold relationship with the Spirit of God. Jesus had said to them in John, that the Holy Ghost would be sent to them as a Helper. He told them, *"He dwells with you and will be in you"* (NKJV, John 14:16-17) So the Holy Ghost had already been with them, but Jesus said that in the future He would be in them. Then in Acts, He said, *"But you shall receive power when the Holy Ghost has come upon you"* (Acts 1:8). So the Holy Ghost was always with them. Now He came into them as Jesus breathed on them. This was their spiritual birth as they experienced the indwelling of the Holy Ghost.

If you have never accepted Jesus Christ as your Savior, the Holy Ghost is there with you, to draw you to God and to convict you in godly sorrow of sin. However if you have accepted Jesus, then the Holy Ghost is inside you and you've been born again. *"For as many as received Him to them He gave the power (right) to become children of God..."* (Jn. 1:12).

But He wants to come upon you and fill your heart, to give you the power to live a godly life. But it was on the Day of Pentecost when they were all filled with the power of the Holy Ghost which comes upon a believer for service.

Please don't stop short of all that God has for you. Ask and you shall receive the power of the Spirit to fill you with His joy. Everyone has a vacuum deep down inside the core of their being that cries out for satisfaction. There are people who are trying to fill this spiritual thirst with physical things. It just doesn't work. You end up thirstier. There are others who try to satisfy that thirst with emotional experiences, but that to leaves you dry.

Deep down inside us, we all have a thirst that can only be quenched by a personal relationship with God. My friend, it is my prayer that you will take time this day and pray that God will fill you with His Holy Spirit that you may draw from the Well that never shall run dry.

Chapter 3
Vision Through The Eyes Of Faith

☙❧

I've noticed as I have grown older a need to get an upgrade to my prescription eyeglasses. My vision is not the same as it was several years ago. Yes it's time for an upgrade. But what happens when we need to upgrade our eyeglasses and do nothing about it? Our vision can become seriously impaired. And the chances of an accident while driving increases dramatically depending on how impaired it is. Not only do I put myself at risk, but everyone who's riding with me. Yes, I may be visually impaired.

Now let us look at it from a character standpoint. I call it poor "I-sight." At each end of the spectrum, we find an unhealthy extreme of "I-sight." At one end we have self-love (narcissism), and at the other end we have self-hatred; self-elevation, and then self-condemnation. We drive others away, while swinging from one side to the other promotions and demotions, on a see-saw of ups and downs. We rise, only to be lowered again, back and forth, around and around. One day, I'm too high on self and the next day I'm too hard on myself. I see myself and I don't like what I see. "O wretched man that I am! Who will deliver me from this body of death?" (Rom. 7:24). Well, neither view is correct.

Where! O where then is the truth? Right there in the middle—dead center between "I can do anything" and "I can't do anything at all" lies the critical key… "I can do all things through Christ who strengthens me" (Phil. 4:13).

I'm neither superman nor Clark Kent. I am not self-secure, nor am I insecure, but Christ-secure: a self-worth based in our identity as children of God. My friend, the proper prescription for "I-sight" is in God's love for me in Christ. "Behold what manner of love the Father has bestowed on us that we should be called the children of God!" (1 John 3:1).

Dreams and Visions
When the Holy Spirit was poured out on the Church at Pentecost, Peter said that the events that occurred were a fulfillment of what had been spoken by the Prophet Joel, *"And it shall come to pass afterward that I will pour out My Spirit on all flesh; Your sons and your daughters shall prophesy, Your old men shall dream dreams, your young men shall see visions And also on My menservants and on My maidservants I will pour out My Spirit in those days;"* (Joel 2:28-29).

When God speaks, He often does so through dreams as given to Daniel, Joseph, Jacob, Gideon, and visions as those given to Abraham, Samuel, Job, Isaiah, Ezekiel, Daniel, Zechariah, and Apostle Paul. Visions are much like dreams. The difference is dreams are usually experienced during sleep, while vision can be seen while asleep or awake, as if in a trance. And then it is possible to experience a vision within a dream, as was the case of Nebuchadnezzar, King of Babylon (Daniel 2:4).

The Word of God has much to say about dreams and visions. Dreams are mentioned about 122 times in the Bible, and visions are mentioned about 101 times. A vision is a gift where you can see into the spiritual realm. The Hebrew word for "vision" when translated has several meanings: (1) a view, (2) an appearance, and (3) a shape; in the noun tense it means "a dream, revelation, oracle, a sight, or a striking appearance; in the verb tense it means "to gaze at, mentally perceive, behold, prophesy, or to see." In the Old Testament, we find this gift exercised many times by the prophets.

Vision Through The Eyes of Faith

The prophet Ezekiel saw the throne of God (Ez. 1:26). Daniel dreamed dreams that deeply disturbed him, and saw visions of the Ancient of Days, the Almighty God coming in great glory (Dan. 2:44; 8:27). God in His sovereignty has also given dreams and visions to laymen.

It is critical and of utmost importance that when there are spiritual manifestations or phenomena taking place, we are able to give people a scriptural basis for what is happening. Whether it is a psychological or metaphysical phenomenon, unless there is solid scriptural basis for it, you are treading on dangerous ground to label it as coming from God. We cannot use experience alone as criterion for truth because people come along with all kinds of strange and weird experiences. I believe that the Holy Scriptures are the final authority and the foundation for truth. If we stand on the scriptures, we stand on the truth.

The individual who mentally visualizes himself achieving as opposed to failing, and is willing to pay the price of diligent, sustained effort, advances steadily toward his goal. Mental vision is vital, for what we become is closely related to our self-image—how we view ourselves. What we think and what we visualize to a large degree is what we become. The Apostle Paul states *"And be not conformed to this world, but be you transformed by the renewing of your mind..."* (Romans 12:2)

The Object of Our Hope

I believe that one of the greatest needs that we have today is the need for hope. Dr. McNair Wilson, renowned cardiologist, states in his autobiography Doctor's Progress, *"Hope is the medicine I use more than any other—hope can cure nearly anything."* Emil Brunner once said, *"What oxygen is to the lungs, such is hope to the meaning of life."* Hope contemplates the future and expects the good. Hope is a state of mind that causes me to look forward to some desire with expectation or as the source of or reason for such a hope.

By today's standard, we seem to put less emphasis on the "expectation" component of hope. "I hope it doesn't snow tomorrow—but I'm getting my snow blower ready just in case." "I hope the Vikings win the Super Bowl this year, but I've been wishing that every year for the last twenty-five years." We still look forward to a desired end, but we don't stake our lives on whether or not it will happen, because the thing hoped for is uncertain at best. As a matter of fact, this kind of hope often carries the unfilled expectations as we look forward to desires, but in heart we're viewing them as remote possibilities. Then our hope tends to be feeble and desperate. Perhaps it's because we as a society have become like those Apostle Paul described in Ephesians 2:12 who are separated from Christ and consequently have no hope.

But hope in God's Word is different. It is certain, a confident expectation of what God will do in the future based on His past faithfulness and promises. It is certain because of who God is. God is faithful, and His Word is trustworthy. He is a constant friend and the only constantly reliable source for our hope. This kind of hope is solid and dependable, *"an anchor for the soul, sure and strong"* (Heb. 6:19).

Apostle Paul in Ephesians, Chapter Six, stresses the importance of putting on the whole armor of God. He mentions two particular items, the breastplate of righteousness which protects the heart, and the helmet of salvation which protects the head. We know that the head houses among things the mind. In effect, he speaks about of the helmet as protection for our minds. If a soldier in battle is wounded in the head, he may not be able to make effective use of his equipment. He may otherwise be a very brave and skilled soldier and armed with the best equipment, but when he is wounded in the head, it becomes very difficult for him to make effective use of his equipment. He may turn on his comrade in arms, confusing friend with foe. This is true of many Christians today when we allow ourselves to become prey to depression or to mistrust other Christian workers. This problem in the mind may prevent us from being the kind of servants that God wants us to be.

Vision Through The Eyes of Faith

Paul was writing to the Saints in Ephesus when he said, *"Put on the helmet of salvation."* (Ephesians 6:17) In 1 Thessalonians we find a parallel passage, *"But let us, who are of the day, be sober, putting on the breastplate of faith and love; and as a helmet, the hope of salvation."* (1 Thessalonians 5:8) The protection for the mind is hope, but the protection for the heart is faith. *"With the heart man believes unto righteousness."* (Romans 10:10)

What is the connection between faith and hope? Hebrews says, *"Now faith is the substance of things hoped for. ..."* (Hebrews 11:1) Faith is the foundation upon which hope is built. When our faith is valid, then our hope is true which yields vital protection for the mind. According to the scriptures, hope is a quiet, steady anticipation of good based on God's Word. It's the fuel that drives optimism. Hope is an optimistic attitude that always chooses to see the best and will never surrender to depression, doubt, despair, or self-pity. Simply said, hope never gives up and never gives in. says, *"For we are saved by hope..."* (Romans 8:24)

In the Old Testament, God Himself was the foundation and object of hope. When God fulfilled His promise to Abraham, He delivered the Israelites from bondage in Egypt, provided for their needs in the wilderness and formed them into a covenant community at Mount Sinai. He then led them into a successful occupation in the land of Canaan, providing a firm base for their faith in Him as He continued His purpose for them.

From Genesis to Revelation, from man's greatest tragedy (the fall) to his greatest triumph, we find that God's dramatic solution summed up in the words of our Lord Jesus, *"For God so loved the world, that He gave His only begotten Son, that whosoever believeth in Him should not perish, but have everlasting life"* (Jn. 3:16). These life changing words are filled with tremendous power for the hopeless and those sitting in the shadows of death.

Discernment

There is a Persian proverb that sounds more like a tongue twister than sound advice:

Knows and Knows Not

He who knows not, and knows not that he knows not, is a fool---shun him.
He who knows not, and knows that he knows not, is a child---teach him.
He who knows, and knows not that he knows, is asleep
---wake him.
He who knows and knows that he knows, is wise ---follow him.

All four "types" can be found on every campus, in any business, among all neighborhoods, within every church. They may not wear badges that say "I'm a fool." Nor do they introduce themselves accordingly. You'll never have someone walk up, shake your hand, and say, "Hi, I'm Dan. I'm a fool." Chances are good that the last thing he will want you to discover is the deep-down truth that "he knows not that he knows not."

Then how in the world are we to know whom to shun, to teach, to awaken, or to follow? Discernment is the answer—skill and accuracy in reading character and the ability to detect and identify the real truth, to see beneath the surface and correctly "size up" the situation, to read between the lines.

When God told Solomon to ask what he wanted from God, the king responded, *"...give thy servant an understanding heart to judge Thy people; to discern between good and evil"* (1 Kings 3:9). He had expressed with humility his own lack of experience and ability to govern the people. The word that is translated "understanding" is the Hebrew word "Binah" which means "listening." Solomon was asking for a heart of wisdom—a heart that listens to people and hears from God. This is the right answer to the question, "What do you want?" This should be our desire over and above everything else. God was so pleased with his answer that He said He would not only make Solomon the wisest man in the world, but He would also give him riches and honor because he didn't ask for them. We are assured in James 1:5 that God will give wisdom to anyone who asks.

And who doesn't know about the "wisdom" of Solomon to this very day? The Apostle Paul tells us that discernment is one characteristic that goes hand-in-hand with genuine spirituality (1 Cor. 2:14-16). Hebrews calls it a mark of maturity. (Hebrews 5:14) Discernment gives to us a proper frame of reference, a definite line, separating good and evil. It acts as an umpire in life and blows the whistle on that which is false. It's as particular as a pathologist peering into a microscope and it never falls for foolish fakes; it never flirts with masquerading phonies, or dances with deceivers or kisses counterfeiting cons goodnight.

You see, discernment would rather rest in the Lord and wait patiently for Him than to mess around with gullible gangbusters. It's from the Word of God that we learn to distinguish the fools from the wise. John the apostle wrote, *"Beloved, believe not every spirit, but test the spirits, whether they are of God..."* (1 Jn. 4:1). Simply put, stop believing everything you hear, and quit being so easily convinced. Be selective. Think. Discern! Love without discernment is an open invitation to all kinds of heresies and false doctrines. A person without discernment is like a submarine in a harbor plowing full speed ahead without a radar or periscope. Imagine a 747 Jumbo Jet trying to land in a fog without instruments or radio. There's lots of noise and a great deal of power. The pilot has good intentions until the unthinkable happens.

You say you want wisdom, but you don't know where to go to find it? First, go to God in prayer, remembering that in James 1:5, God promises wisdom to those who ask for it. Then go to the Word of God. Psalm 119:98-100, offer tremendous insight concerning wisdom. This offer is good throughout life and comes with a satisfaction guaranteed clause. All may apply, even those who think they know it all, and know not that they know nothing.

In knowledge I know about God. Knowledge gives me an awareness of God and information of the fact that God exists. But wisdom is the ability to judge what I know. Wisdom knows what to do with that knowledge. Have you ever heard the expression; "I see what you mean," that's understanding what you've heard.

There is a difference between knowing about God and really comprehending and seeing God. How do we differentiate between the two? That is the position of so many today. They really don't know God. They've heard about God. However, just hearing about God will not change your lifestyle. You still live as though God does not exist. You never give any time to God. You may say, "Sure, I believe in God. I've heard the preacher up the street talk about God. Oh, yes, I believe there is a God." But the life you live tells a different story; that you have never seen God, nor submitted yourself to Him. Have you ever sought His counsel or His guidance? He has never really been an important part of your life. Job said, *"I have heard about You by the hearing of the ear, but now my eyes see You."* (Job 42:5) And, as a result of really seeing God, or the truth of God, the effect was so profound that he uttered, *"I abhor myself. I repent in dust and ashes"* (Job 42:6).

I grew up in a Christian home. I heard about God, went to church on Sundays. When the minister prayed I'd bow my head in reverence to God, but didn't know Him. Late in the evening I would sit on my front porch and sing sad love songs; longing for "my Cherie Amore." Where was she? Who was she? Who could love a wretched sinner like me. It was the absence of love that broke my heart. I heard that God could save me, but I wanted someone to love. My nights were restless, often sleepless. Was I truly less of a man then other men. Isn't it funny how we tend to judge ourselves by someone else's standard of who we are. Well, it was not until I came to Jesus that I saw God and I found true love in Him.

A Matter of Perspective

By resting in the letter of the Law and shutting their eyes to the light, the Jews became blind to the fact that the old covenant was abolished and done away. They had a veil over their eyes from the time of Moses and couldn't see the Lord clearly. Many Christians are just as blind to the same simple truth because of the belief that the Ten Commandments are still in force as a requirement to obtain righteousness. But the veil has been lifted for us; and as we see Him, (Christ) we *"are being transformed into the same image from glory to glory, just as by the Spirit of the Lord."* (2 Cor 3:) When the Jews turn to God through Christ, this blindness will be taken away (2 Cor. 3:16). Adam was originally created in the image of God, but the image was distorted by his fall. Now it is God's desire to restore us back into His image as we behold the glory of Jesus (2 Cor. 3:18).

Peter had spent most of the night fishing. But he hadn't caught anything. Jesus said to Peter to head out into deeper water, and although he thought it seemed useless, he obeyed just to humor the Lord. However much to the surprise of Peter and those with him, they caught so many fish that their boats began to sink. As the boats were sinking, it began to sink into Peter's consciousness just who Jesus really was. He realized that Jesus was no ordinary man, but He was in fact the Messiah. But as he recognized Jesus for who He was, Peter also saw himself for who he was. He said, *"Depart from me, for I am a sinful man, O Lord!"* (Lk. 5:5-8).

Whenever we get a vision of who Jesus really is, it will also give us a practical perspective of who we really are as well. We fail to see ourselves in the light of His glory. This always brings positive conviction, healing and transformation.

When we try to understand the vicissitudes of life in the framework of daily temporal existence, we're not going to understand the plan of God as He works in our lives; because God doesn't work in our lives just for the temporary benefit. As God is looking at you, He is absolutely, entirely concerned about you. And as God is working in your life, He's looking at the eternal benefits.

Let's say, you want to make an investment today that's going to pay dividends tomorrow. Well, God has made an investment in you, and the things He is doing in you are for the eternal dividends, for your eternal welfare, your eternal good. In order to understand them, I must see them as they relate to eternity in order to understand them. The Psalmist said it so well, *"When I thought how to understand this, it was too painful for me—until I went into the sanctuary of God; then I understood their end"* (Ps. 73:16,17). When I saw it in the eternal framework, then I could see it clearly, the eternal perspective.

You may be going through a time of suffering or a time of pain, but remember, as Apostle Paul said, *"For our light affliction, which is but for a moment, is working a far more exceeding and eternal weight of glory"* (2 Cor. 4:17).

Jacob was "caught in the squeeze"—he was "caught between a rock and a hard place." His perspective was his problem, or as far as he could see, upon the return of his sons from Egypt, where they had gone to buy grain. "It happened as they had emptied their sacks, that surprisingly each man's bundle of money was in his sack; and when they and their father saw the bundles of money, they were afraid. And Jacob their father said to them, *"You have bereaved me: Joseph is no more, Simeon is no more, and you want to take Benjamin. All these things are against me"* (Gen. 42:35,36).

As far as Jacob could see, this was a problem—he was shortsighted. We also like Jacob, with our limited vision and inability to see past today, look at the circumstances of our life and conclude, "Everything is going against me."

When you are prone to cry out, "All things are against me," this is never the case in reality. My friend, you don't know all things. At best, you only know part of the things. One of our problems is our narrow view of things. Peter said we cannot see afar off. We only see that which is near, that which is close. And you're making a judgment on the basis of incomplete knowledge. God oftentimes is working out His plan in our lives that are not going to come to fruition until years down the road. He has this entire process all worked out and years from now it will flourish. *"All things work together for good to those who love God, to those who are called according to His purpose"* (Rom. 8:28). So we must wait until all of the facts are in, and you'll see it differently, with a new perspective. Wait for the Lord! Attend upon Him—a new chapter is about to begin; you'll see the completion of God's plan unfold and realize that it is far different from what it appears to be at the present.

Jacob came to understand in time that his son Joseph, whom he thought was dead, was not only alive, but was now in fact the Prime Minister of all Egypt. And as he looked back in retrospect, he realized that all the while God's hand was on his son. God wanted to preserve the family, so He sent Joseph ahead to prepare the place (Gen. 50:19-20). Let's take a look at Joseph's ordeal as he was heading out on that caravan, after being sold into slavery by his brothers: as he was crying and looking back, he saw their selfish greed as they were dividing the money. He had to be wondering, "Where is God?"

Imagine Joseph being taken down to Egypt, and Potiphar an officer of Pharaoh, captain of the guard, an Egyptian, who brings him from the Ishmaelites who had taken him there. Here he was sold into slavery and to add insult to injury, his master's wife finds him irresistible…*"Lie with me, no one will know—there's no one else here in the house but you and I."* (Gen. 39:12) As Joseph flees, she catches hold and strips him of his outer garment, but he doesn't look back. Now as a woman scorned, she waits for the return of her husband and cries, *"He tried to rape me; and when I lifted my voice and cried out, he left his garment with me and fled outside."* (Gen. 39:14) Consequently, he's thrown into prison for a crime he did not commit. Listen closely—can you hear him echoing

… "Where is God?"

Let's recapitulate for a moment. Remember whenever you are prone in your circumstances to cry, "Everything is against me, God must be against me, and God doesn't love me" it is then that we must trust that all things are working together for the good of those who love the Lord; to those who are called according to His purpose. Do you love Him? Then what shall we say to these things? If God be for us: who can be against us.

Look Through the Eyes of Faith
In 2 Kings, the Syrian army had surrounded Elisha, and his servant was terrified. Elisha prayed, *"Lord, I pray, open his [the servant] eyes that he may see."* (2 Kings 6:17) The young man's eyes were opened, and he saw that the Syrians were completely surrounded by angelic forces. Elisha said that *"those who are with us are more than those who are with them."* (2 Kings 6:16) There is an unseen spiritual realm of which we are normally unaware. We get so involved in the physical realm of every day living that we often lose sight of the spiritual realm. When we focus only on the physical things, we can see it is easy for us to lose hope and become discouraged, thinking there is no way we can ever win.

Isaiah states, *"In the year that King Uzziah died, I saw the Lord sitting on a throne, high and lifted up, and the train of His robe filled the temple."* (Isaiah 6:1)

Uzziah was a very powerful king of Judah. Under his reign the people felt safe and secure. The people were prospering in a time of peace. But we learn in 2 Chronicles, that *"when he was strong, his heart was lifted up to his destruction."* (2 Chronicles 26:16)

Times of prosperity can be more dangerous than times of poverty. When we are successful, as God works through our lives in marvelous ways, we must continue to walk humbly before Him. But if we become confident in our own flesh, our confidence is often based on our own capacities rather than on the power of God. This is where the danger come in as *"Pride goes before destruction, and a haughty spirit before a fall"* (Prov. 16:18). When we are strong we must not let our success lead us to feel that we can survive independent from God. This kind of mentality will lead us to stray into areas where we should never go and to presumptuously take on roles to which we are not called.

Uzziah thought he was above God's law as he dabbled in the priestly calling. Such thinking proved disastrous for it cost him his health as he came down with leprosy and ultimately death. The people trusted in Uzziah and when he died they were crushed and distraught. But that was when the vision of the Lord was revealed to the prophet Isaiah sitting upon His throne.

Sometimes God has to remove our heroes so that we can see Him. He wants us to see His glory. And that it's not about what we want, but about Him; that He is on the throne. What am I going to do now? So many have asked this question when someone or something dear to them has died. And at the time of their desperation they see the Lord. A man was asked, "How did you come to Christ?" His reply was, "I was standing at the gravesite of my little girl, and as I watched the casket being lowered into the ground, I saw the Lord. He was knocking on the door of my heart. I opened the door and let Him in."

We need to see the Lord. Anything that obstructs our view of Him needs to die so that we can see Him, high and lifted up. When we see Jesus Christ, we realize all our righteousness is as filthy rags and that only His blood can make us clean.

In the natural, our enemies seem to have so much more power than we do. But the Word of God tells us, *"He who is in you is greater than he who is in the world"* (1 Jn. 4:4b). But we sometimes forget this and start to panic. May God give us eyes of faith; that we might see in the spirit. What a difference it would make in our whole outlook when we see through the eyes of faith.

Chapter 4
Showers of Mercy

☙❧

Breath of God

Oh Morning Breeze,
Through rustling trees.
From green grass new,
To garden fresh.
Whistling under eagle's wing,
A song and dance to creation's King.

Dost thou know, of long ago?
East Wind blew upon a sea of Red.
Many found his terror, in the face of dread.
To open gates of freedom by his Master's hand.
Onward through a wilderness,
To a land of promise.

Dost thou know?
Four winds which blew.
To raise again, to snatch from death, the slain.
Because of sin, they lie within,
Death's valley, dark and low.
Was it mercy's friend, who then began to blow?
Was it Love who blew?
I heard the Breath of God did too.

Hope For A Troubled Heart

To this end, that those once dead would live again,
I heard the Breath of God did blow.
Oh, Morning Breeze, now hear my sigh.
Lift now my prayer,
Beyond this mountain high.
To my Father's throne.
A mother dies inside alone
You see twas yesterday, her ecstasy.
Can you see the falling rain,
Tears like rain.
Or feel her soul's despair.
Behold, a mother's pain,
Behold, a mother's agony,
Please hear, Mercy weep.

Oh, Breath of God,
Hear my plea.
Her lullaby, now a song of dread.
Oh, breathe upon these slain.
Young men, brave hearts,
Sun crowned, Black men,
Slain by sin.
Tyranny has raised his gruesome head.

Does now justice sleep?
A house is not a home,
As long as mother's weep.
Breath Of God

Wes Belfrey (1980)

O LORD, I have heard thy speech, and was afraid: O LORD, revive Thy work in the midst of the years, in the midst of the years make known; in wrath remember mercy (Hab. 3:2).

Showers of Mercy

Habakkuk's song is wonderful; it is a beautiful prayer. Habakkuk says, *"O Lord, I have heard Thy speech."* (Hab. 3:2) God answered him in so many words … *"You think that I am not doing anything about the sins of My people, but I am. I am preparing a nation, but when I am through with the Chaldeans, I am going to judge them, and I will judge them on a righteous basis."* (Hab. 1:6) God was moving to bring Babylon down.

The interesting thing is that Habakkuk now reverses his plea—a reversal has taken place in Habakkuk's thinking. At first he said, *"You are not doing anything, Lord." Why don't You do something? Why do You let them get by with their sin?"* (Hab. 1:2-4). God has let Habakkuk know that He is doing something, and Habakkuk cries out for mercy. What is he now afraid of? Well, now he is afraid of the Lord doing too much!

Well, God is merciful, and God is gracious. He is not willing that any should perish.

Habakkuk's prayer is actually a recital of what God has done in the past history of Israel. In view of the fact that He has done it in the past, He intends for God to do it again in the future. You can depend upon God's continuing to do what He has done in the past. This is our confidence, and this is the confidence of this psalm of Habakkuk.

It may look today as if God is not doing anything, but if we could ascend to the watchtower of Habakkuk, if we could learn that the just shall live by faith, if we could have a living faith in God and see what is going on behind the scenes and see the wheels of judgment that are turning, I think we would be just as surprised as Habakkuk was. I am sure that we too would cry out to God for mercy. A great many of us today have thrown up our hands and given up on the state of our nation. We all have felt this way at one time or another. But God is a God of judgment and He is moving today in judgment, and somebody needs to cry out to Him, and say "O, Lord, in wrath, as You are moving in judgment, please don't forget to be merciful to us. We need Your mercy."

This great nation of ours needs the mercy of God. What would we do in the time of a major crisis? I am not a pessimist, but what if there was another terrorist attack? How much gasoline would there be? How long would we last without the mercy of God? I believe that God is moving in judgment and we need to ask Him to be merciful to us. We often talk about showers of blessing—what we need today are showers of mercy from God Almighty.

Shakespeare has Portia say in The Merchant of Venice (Act 1V, Scene I):

> *The quality of mercy is not strain'd,*
> *It droppeth as the gentle rain from heaven*
> *Upon the place beneath. It is twice blest:*
> *It blesseth him that gives and him that takes.*

Mercy is a characteristic that comes straight from the very nature of God. When we consider the condition and needs of others, we are acting in His mercy. It In the Old Testament, God's mercy was not primarily extended to those outside His covenant community, but was is a necessary temperament of God's people. expressed mainly towards His people Israel. It also became the expected attitude and action of the people of Israel towards each other. Today God has passed this expectation of mercy on to the Church and has become a chief rule in the life of every believer. Our Lord made it a fundamental part of His Christian manifesto in the Sermon on the Mount (Matt. 5:7). Mercy is an action taken by the strong towards the weak, the wealthy towards the poor, the compassionate towards the needy, the mighty towards the destitute, those who have towards those who have not.

The mercy of God is the foundation of forgiveness. It is His faithfulness and steadfast love. In His mercy, God made continual provision for Israel such as manna in the wilderness (Ex. 16:4-5), or as their Shepherd of their protection, who keeps Israel and does not sleep in Psalm, Chapter 121. Mercy has never been the benefit of God's people as based upon their

Showers of Mercy

worth, but is always the gift of God—*"The LORD, The LORD God, merciful and gracious, longsuffering, and abounding in goodness and truth, keeping mercy for thousands, forgiving iniquity and transgression and sin"* (Ex. 34:6,7).

People are ordinary at best and we should be concerned about other's issues—heartaches, hunger, sickness, shattered lives, insecurities; and as human beings, we are all subject to failure and grief. Are these only to be viewed as temporary problems, mere horizontal hassles of the human kind?

Some of you may say, "Hey Wes, leave that to the liberals. Our job is to give them the gospel—to get them saved! Don't be sidetracked by their pain and suffering." But as Jesus went about preaching the gospel, He allowed Himself to be sidetracked by the cry of a leper. *"And behold, a leper came and worshiped Him saying, 'Lord, if You are willing, You can make me clean.' And Jesus put out His hand and touched him, saying, 'I am willing; be cleansed.' Immediately his leprosy was cleansed"* (Matt. 8:2,3).

When our children were small, sometimes we would take them to Valley Fair, an Amusement Park in Shakopee, Minnesota. I remember on one occasion people started running toward the front entrance. So I asked a staff person, "Hey, what's going on?" He replied, "There's a tornado, and it's heading in our direction. Please go to the designated area for shelter." We were instructed to go to an area which slopped into a lower level of landscape. And as we all gathered sitting along the crest of a trench, I can recall an eerie feeling as the winds began to blow. Suddenly someone on a bull horn cried out, "Everybody get down! We are in the path of a tornado, please get down!" Panic ensued, people ran, they wept, some screamed. My sister-in-law who was with us that day grabbed me by my jacket with a look of shear terror as she cried out, "You're a minister, pray!!" I don't think I was afraid until then. But as I bowed over my son Chris, covering him with my body and Delores covering our baby girl Christine, I called on the Lord. With eyes closed, face to the ground, and heart pounding, I cried, "O Lord, Your furious winds make me afraid, and cause me to fear. Let thy angel encamp about us and let the tornado pass, let the storm pass over us. And God answered me. I can still here Him saying, "Don't be afraid; be of good cheer—I am with you."

Have you ever prayed and you wanted to make sure God heard you, so you prayed again. And so I did, "But God, I'm really afraid, O let your angel protect us and let the storm pass over us!" I'm sure that I was not the only one praying, but I thank God because just before it touched down, the tornado passed over. He heard our prayer. I thank God He had mercy on us.

> *But I will have mercy upon the house of Judah, and will save them by the Lord their God, and will not save them by bow, nor by sword, nor by battle, by horses, nor by horsemen.*
>
> (Hos. 1:7)

There has always been the question as to the possibility of a person stepping over a line—that is, sinking so low in sin that the mercy of God cannot reach him. While I do not believe that you could ever get to a place where God by His mercy and grace could not save you, I do believe that if you persist in rejecting God's grace and mercy, the day will come when you will step over that line. This does not mean the mercy of God cannot reach you, but it does mean there will be nothing in you that the mercy of God can lay hold of. Many people take the mercy of God for granted. However you can trifle with God too long. The nation of Israel did and the day came when God said, *"I will no longer have mercy on you."* (Hos. 1:6)

However, concerning Judah God said, *"I am not ready yet to judge the house of Judah."* (Hos. 1:7) Why will He spare Judah and not Israel? It was for the sake of David. God had said that for the sake of David, He would not divide the kingdom under the reign of Solomon. Again and again God said this for the sake of David. He would save the southern kingdom. Someone may want to criticize this and say that doesn't sound fair. I don't know whether it is, but I thank God that He had mercy on me, and that He was patient and gracious, and continues to show mercy even to this very day. God is a God of mercy.

Matthew states, *"Blessed are the merciful, for they shall obtain mercy."* (Mathew 5:7) As we recognize our own need for mercy, we begin to show mercy. And showing mercy has a cleansing effect on our lives. We sing Amazing Grace, but God's mercy is amazing as well. Whereas grace is the unearned favor of the love of God, mercy is a negative, which is not getting the justice we deserve. When justice says, Thou shall die, for you have sinned, it is mercy that objects. Mercy says No! pointing to the blood of Jesus—then justice has to concede.

The Day Mercy Said "No"

I believe that God has an unseen hand of mercy. Years ago, as a youngster living in Southern California, my friend Phillip came over one day and said, "Wesley come on. Let's go. Today we're going to find you that puppy Doberman Pincher you've been talking about." So we walked down the street, around the corner, out of our hood and into another. As boys in the hood we should have known better. It was a hot summer day and there we were; walking by a house with a number of gang members. Some were standing, others sitting around on the lawn, but all eyes were on us. I had an eerie feeling, as though something bad was about to happen. They stopped talking, stopped laughing and I knew that we were in the wrong place at the wrong time. We turned the corner and started up the alley when much to our dismay, there they were coming, like soldiers marching into battle. I could hear thunder in their steps. Terror was on the attack and I was their prey. The roar of the pack sent shivers down my spine. "Was this the day of my demise"?

Hope For A Troubled Heart

As we slowly turned around we faced yet another group coming in from the other entrance of the alley. I tried to be calm, but couldn't stop my knees from shaking. Suddenly Phillip made a mad dash for a backyard fence nearby, and with those long legs he was up, over, and out of sight. "Get em. Get em! get that little motha…" they yelled as they rushed toward me. And I let out a goat wrenching scream, "mama" as I attempted to scale the nearest fence, I found myself sliding back down. But knowing it was now or never, I jumped again, and it was as if an invisible hand gave me a boost, and over I went. Looking over my shoulder, I noticed this big brother on my heels coming over after me. "Get him, get him!" they cried. I dashed for the side gate of the back yard, and as I opened the latch out of the garage came flying another terror—a monstrosity of a dog; a huge German Shepherd snapping for my arm. But once again, mercy showed up and not a minute too soon; for he was at the end of his leash, just inches away, just before he could clamp those vice grip like jaws around me.

Wow! Talking about an adrenaline rush!! Well, what happened to the guy who was coming over after me? When he saw that monstrosity of a dog; back over he went, on the other side, and like "a bat out of hell," I was off in a flash—across the street on the side of the nearest house I could find. I huddled down behind a bush shaking like a leaf. My heart pounding in fear—"Did he see me," I wondered did he see me?" I watched while an elderly gentleman came out of the front door of the house. He released his dog and it began sniffing the ground as though trying to pick up my scent. I waited until they were down the street and out of sight before leaving. I remember looking up to heaven that day and saying, "Somebody up there must like me!" I was still alive!

Sometimes I still think about it. How in the world did I get over that fence? Did God, in His mercy send an angel to deliver me? I believe so. In Psalm 51, we see a prayer of repentance. David prayed after being confronted by Nathan the prophet with his sin of adultery with Bathsheba and the murder of her husband Uriah. There is so much we can learn from this prayer.

As a young man, David would sometimes cry out to God for justice to be done. Now as an older, wiser man, he cried for mercy. He acknowledged that his sin was always before God and that all sin is against God. He also recognized the need for his heart to be cleansed and for his relationship with the Holy Spirit to be restored. David had lost the joy of his salvation and he wanted it back. He knew that God wasn't after sacrifice, but a broken and contrite heart. And he intended to teach others about the folly of sin and the need to walk in righteousness.

The Prophet Jeremiah was another who was devastated by the knowledge of God's judgment that was about to fall upon His people. Yet in the midst of all the chaos, he began to think on the Lord. He remembered God's mercy and the fact that we would have been consumed long ago if it were not for His mercy. He remembered God's compassions that are new every morning. He acknowledged the faithfulness and goodness of God. And he realized that God was the only hope of salvation.

This I recall to mind, therefore I have hope. Through the Lord's mercies we are not consumed, because His compassions fail not. They are new every morning; Great is Your faithfulness. "The Lord is my portion," says my soul, "Therefore I hope in Him!" The Lord is good to those who wait for Him, to the soul who seeks Him. It is good that one should hope and wait quietly for the salvation of the Lord (Lam. 3:21-26).

The God of a Second Chance
I believe God is a God of second chances.

The Angel of the Lord said unto Samson's mother, *"You shall conceive and bear a son. Now therefore, please be careful not to drink wine or similar drink, and not to eat anything unclean. For behold, you shall conceive and bear a son. And no razor shall come upon his head, for the child shall be a Nazarite to God from the womb; and he shall begin to deliver Israel out of the hand of the Philistines"* (Jud. 13:3-5)

Years passed and Samson became a young man. And in the sixteenth chapter, verse four we find that he loved a woman in the Valley of Sorek, whose name was Delilah. And the lords of the Philistines came up to her and said to her, *"Entice him, and find out where his great strength lies, and by what means we may overpower him, that we may bind him to afflict him; and everyone of us will give you eleven hundred pieces of silver."* (Jud. 16:5)

It's sad to see how Samson so foolishly allowed himself to be brought down and caught in the clutches of this woman. It came to pass that when she had pestered him daily with her words and pressed him, so that his soul was vexed to death, that he told her all his heart … *"No razor has ever come upon my head, for I have been a Nazarite to God from my mother's womb. If I am shaven, then my strength will leave me, and I shall become weak, and be like any other man."* (Jud. 16:17)

Samson now blinded by his sin, continues his fall into her trap, for when Delilah saw that he had told her all his heart, she sent and called for the lords of the Philistines. Then she lulled him to sleep on her knees and called for a man to shave off the seven locks of his head. It was a cat and mouse game, a tit for tat, and the rats under a cloak of darkness waited to pounce upon their prey. Then the Philistines took him and put out his eyes, and brought him down to Gaza. They bound him with bronze fetters, and he became a grinder in the prison. But thank God that is not the end of the story.

After Samson had been enslaved for a period of time, his hair began to grow again. Then in verse twenty-eight, Samson called to the Lord, saying, *"O Lord GOD, remember me, I pray! Strengthen me, I pray, just this once, O God…"* (Jud. 16:28) He then was given the strength from God to defeat his enemies. God heard Samson's cry because He is full of mercy and He is the God of a second chance.

We spent Saturday night at Mrs. Alford's house. Her son Therin and I were best of friends. The next morning we

Showers of Mercy

headed for Will Rogers Park; for a day of fun in the sun. It was on a Sunday—Mother's Day. My brothers Louis, Michael, and Therin; were on our way home down Central avenue. Louis and Therin were walking several paces behind Michael and I when suddenly I heard someone shout, "Look out!"

As I turned around, much to my terror, all I could see was this red Chevy Impala heading straight at me—a drunk driver had lost control of his car. I thought, "This couldn't be, I'm on the sidewalk." But there he was, closer and even faster he came. As I turned to run, I felt as though I was moving in slow motion. "Is this a dream? This can't be happening." I think I may have blacked out before impact. The shock was too great for an eleven-year-old, little shorty like me. They say I was thrown in the air like a rag doll as death made its bid for the son of Wesley and Frances Louise Belfrey.

Thankfully, God in His mercy; sparred my life to see the light of another day. The next thing I knew, I awoke to a stranger kneeling over me and removing pieces of concrete which covered my legs—both were broken and one fractured in two places. The driver had evidently smashed into a nearby bus stop bench just before he ran over me. Fanning me with his hat, the passenger of the car said, "Lie still; don't try to move." "Move! What do you mean move," I looked over at my brother Michael, lying underneath the front bumper of the car, and asked "is he dead?" "No" he replied; "he's just unconscious." It seemed as if everything was moving in slow motion and I just wanted to be left alone. Shortly thereafter the ambulance arrived; they pulled out the gurney; "no," don't move me," just let me lie here" if you move me I might break apart," at least that's what I thought. But, of course they did, and rushed me to Central Receiving Hospital. As I recall, my mother upon hearing what happened prayed that God would let me live. It's as if I can still here that awful squeaking sound of burning rubber that could have been the last sound I would ever here on this earth, but I thank God for second chances.

Chapter 5
Trust in God

❦

We face new challenges every day. We become at times overwhelmed by the problems of life. We weep and mourn, as did Jeremiah. Jesus taught that we are to trust God every day to supply our needs, and then He said, "Therefore do not worry about tomorrow, for tomorrow will worry about its own things. Sufficient for the day is its own trouble." As a believer you are not spared life's troubles. Into each life some rain must fall, whether Christian or not. The difference is that we have God's mercy. There is a beautiful hymn based upon this passage of scripture from Lamentations. The lyrics can inspire hope even in the midst of hardship.

> *Great Is Thy Faithfulness*
> *Great is Thy faithfulness, Oh God my Father,*
> *There is no shadow of turning with thee;*
> *Thou changest not, Thy compassions, they fail not,*
> *As Thou hast been Thou forever wilt be.*
>
> *Summer and winter, and springtime and harvest,*
> *Sun, moon, and stars in their courses above,*
> *Join with all nature in manifold witness,*
> *To Thy great faithfulness, mercy and love.*

Hope For A Troubled Heart

Pardon for sin and a peace that endureth,
Thine own dear presence to cheer and to guide;
Strength for today and bright hope for tomorrow,
Blessings all mine, with then thousand beside!

Great is Thy faithfulness!
Great is Thy faithfulness!
Morning by morning new mercies I see;
All I have needed Thy hand hath provided,
Great is Thy faithfulness, Lord unto me!

Thomas O. Chisholm

We need to put God first, at the top of our list of priorities. If we put Him first, He will take care of everything else. Matthew says, *"But seek first the kingdom of God and His righteousness, and all these things will be added to you."* (Mathew 6:33) God knows what you need and He'll take care of your needs. But if you make other things in your life to be the top priorities, you'll find that your life will be out-of-balance. To please God should be the number one goal of our lives—the first purpose of life, the passion that drives us. We need to ask ourselves, what will please the Lord, and then do it. The Bible gives us an example of a man whose life pleased God. The name of that man was Noah. In Noah's day the entire world was filled with moral decay and everyone walked according to their own desire. No one even considered God. But Genesis 6:8, lets us know Noah found grace in the eyes of the Lord—he was a pleasure to the Lord.

Now from Noah's life we see a faith that pleases God. The only way to God is by faith. It's not a gamble; it's not a mystery; it's a "substance" of things hoped for. It's an "evidence" of things not seen. Faith rests on a foundation and that foundation is the Word of God. Spurgeon said: *"It's not thy hold on Christ that saves thee! It's Christ! It's not thy joy in Christ that saves thee! It's Christ!"*

Faith is the instrument that saves you—that is faith in the blood of Christ and His merit that saves you. Faith is that instrument of God that will enable the believer to treat the invisible as seen.

God is pleased when we believe His Word and when we love Him. Noah loved God more than anything. The Bible says that Noah pleased God. He consistently followed God's will and enjoyed a close relationship with Him. God wants a relationship with us. That is what He wants most with us. He wants our fellowship. Yes, God made us to love us and to have us love Him in return. He says: *"I don't want your sacrifices —I want your love; I don't want your offerings —I want you to know me."* (Hos. 6:6)

Secondly, God is pleased when we trust Him. The second reason Noah pleased God was that he trusted God, even when it didn't make sense. The Bible says, *"By faith Noah, being divinely warned of things not yet seen, moved with godly fear, prepared an ark for the saving of his household, by which he condemned the world and became heir of the righteousness which is according to faith."* (Heb. 11:7) He was warned about something he couldn't see, and acted on what he was told. As a result, Noah gained treasured intimacy with Almighty God.

By faith we commit our lives to Christ, but we must trust Him to keep that which we have committed to His care. We trust Him in perilous times, when it seems as though the sun will never shine again. Trust will guard your heart against becoming unthankful in times of stress. Noah preached for one hundred and twenty years before the flood. When laughed at and ridiculed, it was trust in God that kept him building. With only seven workers to help him build, his wife, his three sons and their wives, he kept building. The times were tough, the people were insidious and the days were evil, but he kept on building.

When we see evil people getting away with sin, seemingly without any consequence, it frustrates us, especially when they are doing things against us. But we need to trust in the

Lord. The answer to anxiety, the cure for what's worrying you is trust. God will deal with the wicked, and the wicked will cease from troubling. The wheels of justice may turn seemingly ever so slow, but they grind ever so fine. So why be jealous of them. They will fall and be cut down like grass. And in Psalm, David continues the thought saying not only to *"trust in the Lord,"* but also to *"rest in the Lord."* (Ps. 37:1-3) He will take care of everything.

Job was a man of great patience. He hit rock bottom and his days were dark as night. He lost all of his children in a terrible storm. His wife advised him *"Curse God and die."* (Job 2:9) His friends condemned him: *"You must be guilty of sin."* (Job 22:31) His body was blistered all over with boils. He was being afflicted and he didn't know why. It seemed God had turned against him and all of his friends as well. Here Job probably had reached the lowest point of his life—totally forsaken, it seemed, by both God and man.

But out of this place, this valley of darkness, suddenly Job cried out in faith, words of triumph—probably one of the most triumphant declarations of faith in all of the Old Testament. But it came out of defeat and out of his fears and out of his depression. His cry was prefaced by his desire that these words might be indelibly recorded for posterity. Job cried in Job, *"For I know that my Redeemer lives, and He shall stand at last on the earth; and after my skin is destroyed, this I know, that in my flesh I shall see God."* (Job 19:25) Job in essence was declaring, "Even though the worms may destroy this body, yet in my resurrected body, I shall see God." Talking about trust, Wow! This was indeed a tremendous declaration of faith out of the darkness of Job's circumstances, and of how faith can triumph over defeat. God has placed within the human spirit resilience that cries victory in the face of failure. It is turning our eyes from the situation and unto God. Job did this for a moment. Though his situation seemed hopeless, yet he declared his trust in God ... *"Though He slay me, yet will I trust Him!"* (Job 13:15)

Trust in God

When we go through such circumstances, our problem often stems from the fact that we get so focused and involved in our problem and become so filled with self-pity that all we think about is "Oh, poor me." The more you think about "poor me," the worse off you become. This especially affects our whole mental attitude.

Real faith looks not at the things that are seen, but at the things that are not seen; not at my circumstances, but to God who is greater than my circumstances. One of my favorite hymns says it so well:

> *My Father Watches Over Me*
> *I trust in God wherever I may be,*
> *Upon the land or on the rolling sea,*
> *For, come what may, from day to day,*
> *My heav'nly Father watches over me.*
>
> *He makes the rose an object of His care,*
> *He guides the eagle thru the pathless air,*
> *And surely He remembers me,*
> *My heav'nly Father watches over me.*
>
> *I trust in God, for, in the lion's den,*
> *On battlefield, or in the prison pen,*
> *Thru praise or blame, thru flood or flame,*
> *My heav'nly Father watches over me.*
>
> *The valley may be dark, the shadows deep,*
> *But O, the Shepherd guards His lonely sheep;*
> *And thru the gloom He'll lead me home,*
> *My heav'nly Father watches over me.*

Hope For A Troubled Heart

I trust in God, I know He cares for me,
On mountain bleak or on the stormy sea;
Tho' billows roll, He keeps my soul
My heav'nly Father watches over me.

Rev. W. C. Martin

Maybe you're struggling. And you say, "I am stressed out, and I'm tired of fretting. I am tired of being tired, and so sick of being sick. My life just isn't going the way I want it to." Well, are you feeling that way right now? My friend, you do have legitimate needs and desires. But sometimes we think we know what will make us happy and we may pray earnestly asking God to please grant our prayer. But if it doesn't come to pass, we feel left out, frustrated, disappointed, or even bitter. And we ask God, "Why?"

Delores and I were out house-hunting. We had in mind a four bedroom, two bath house. Our kids were small and we needed something with plenty of room. One day the realtor called and said that he came across something he thought we would like. When we arrived, I was blown away at the sight of it: four bedrooms, two baths, plush carpet, etc. —needless to say, I was too through! In other words, I wanted that house, and I wanted it bad. We prayed, touched and agreed, went through the process, only to discover that someone else, had previously been approved for the loan.

I was devastated asking God why? About four years later we were invited over to a friend of ours. And guess what … yes, it was my dream home. And of course I had to ask, "Queen Esther, what are you doing with my house?" to which she replied, "This house is a nightmare and I am trying my best to sell it, because all throughout the entire house the plumbing is shot." Now think about it. What if God had granted my request? My dream house would have been my nightmare on 42nd & 15th Avenue.

So sometimes we get what we want, only to realize that it didn't make us happy after all, it was just an illusion. It

Trust in God

becomes a crazy merry-go-around; a cycle repeated by many their entire lives, wondering, "What in the world am I doing wrong?"

The answer is not complicated. God offers you freedom from this cycle. He says, "Trust in Me." We must not just say it, but we must do it. You must make it such an important theme in your life that you view every event, every heartache, and every prayer request with the unshakable conviction that God is totally, without question, worthy of our trust. We are prone to trust in things we can see, but by faith we commit our lives to Christ, and then we must trust Him to keep that which we have committed unto Him until God calls us to our heavenly home.

But that's where we miss it. We want to trust in everything and everyone rather than the Lord. We trust in ourselves, our talents, our intellect, our own abilities, in our jobs, in our bank accounts, our doctor or lawyer, but not in the Lord—the most important person of all. The truth is our wants so often do not agree with what God wants for us. After all, it's our life, isn't it? Shouldn't I have the say over it? God gave me a free will, didn't He? Yes, but, I' am responsible for what I do with my freedom.

Well, what does God want? He says in III John; *"Beloved I wish above all things that you may prosper and be in health, even as your soul prospers."* (III John 1:2)

In other words, Gods wants your life to be blessed. His highest wish is for our good.

First, God wants you to have the finances and resources you need in life, but He doesn't want them to have you. He wants whatever you do according to His word to prosper. But you must trust Him to do so. God wants to prosper your spirit, your soul (your mind, your will and your emotions), in your family, in your finances, and in every area of your life. In fact, He wishes it above all things. But we must trust in the Lord and do good. By faith I commit my ways to the Lord. What does it mean to seek first the kingdom of God and all His righteousness? It means to commit my ways over to His way. Then trust Him to provide whatever my needs are. But how do I trust Him with my finances? I work hard for my money. Well, I'm glad you asked,

Knowing who God is opens the door to the blessing of provision.

Abraham the man who the Bible calls the father of all who have faith, (Galatians 3:7), was a man who knew who God was, and he trusted God with his wealth. Melchizedek, a priest of God and king of Salem, blessed him saying; *"Blessed be Abram of the most high God, possessor of heaven and earth: and blessed be the most high God, which has delivered your enemies into your hand."* (Genesis 14:19-20) And he (Abram) gave him tithes of all.

Melchizedek points out four important characteristics of God:

> *He is the most high God.*
> *He is the possessor of heaven and earth.*
> *He is the deliverer from all of our enemies.*
> *He expects us to do our part*
> *and give God tithes of all we have.*

(Genesis 14:18-20)

Madison Avenue type advertising, along with peer pressure tell us what's important: a luxurious automobile, a house on a hill, a six figure income. The fact of the matter is, you were created for something so much better and deep down within, you know it.

Chapter 6
The Love of God

❧

You've had enough of the blues. Haven't you? Enough of the drama! Right? Enough mornings smelling like the mistakes you made while searching for love the night before. Has love's fountain run dry? Has her flame slowly but surely burned out? Leaving nothing but ashes? You've cried a river. Haven't you? And to make matters worse it seems like nobody even cares.

Don't you think it's about time you discover true love? You'll find it on an old rugged tree outside Jerusalem's gate where Jesus hung, Cross-nailed and thorn-crowned. It was intended for mockery, but a crown is actually a sign of victory. It preaches a message of love. Jesus was wearing the consequences of your sin in His death, so that you could gain the victory through His love.

The next time you feel unloved, ascend this mount. Meditate on His love for you. His body soaked with His own blood; His cry to His Father to forgive you. As you stare into the crimsoned face of heaven's only Son, I hope you remember this: *"But God demonstrated His own love toward us, in that while we were still sinners, Christ died for us"* (Rom. 5:8).

Love Light

Shattered dreams say your world is torn apart.
You cry that someone might mend your broken heart.
The music's laughter of yesterday,
The morning after has gone to stay.

Chase the shades of night's despair away.
Turn the midnight into the light of day.
Let Your light shine, Your light Divine.
Upon this heart shine, this heart of mine.

But even when you're in the storm of night,
And it seems like nothing's going right.
A guiding light comes even when you're blue,
Just to warm a broken hearted you.

Love Light,
Let your Light shine;
Warm this cold and wounded heart of mine.
Love is kind, love is true;
O Lord let your Love Light shine.
Love Light.

Wes Belfrey (1994)

"This is love: not that we loved God, but that He loved us and sent His Son as an atoning sacrifice for our sins" (1 John 4:10)

Ever needed a covering in the chill of winter's night? You were sleeping. You didn't know. You tossed and turned until you were without any cover at all. Remember how Mom would enter your room and with tender loving care tuck you in? Maybe it was Dad. But once again you were snug as a bug in a rug.

The Love of God

All of us need a covering. God wants to cover you. Let His love cover all things in your life: all secrets, all fears, all hurts, all hours of loneliness, all hours of darkness, all trouble, all moments of worry, every promise broken, every drug taken, and even every penny stolen, every lie told, and harsh word spoken. His love covers all.

God has a plan for your life. It's a good plan. You were created by God to love and be loved. He loved you in eternity past, before the foundation of the world was ever laid. He loves you with an unconditional love, with an everlasting love. In Jeremiah, the Word of God declares His love for you, *"Yes, I have loved you with an everlasting love; therefore with loving-kindness have I drawn you."* (Jeremiah 31:3) This statement is certainly true for the nation of Israel to whom the prophet was writing, but it is also a truth meant for you to embrace. Yes you.

When the brilliant Swiss theologian Karl Barth was asked by a group of young theologians what was the most important theological fact he had discovered during his lifetime of studies, the old scholar puffed silently on his pipe as he thoughtfully studied the question. The students sat silent in eager anticipation, Finally, he removed his pipe, paused, and simply said, *"Jesus loves me, this I know, for the Bible tells me so!"*

God's love is truly a mystery, but it would not be so if we knew all the answers. We must have faith, for without faith it is impossible to please God. What we do have are the tangible answers God gives us in the revelation of His written Word, and upon that foundation we have the opportunity to share the love of God in Christ Jesus. I believe that love is the most important word in the Bible.

The Law of First Mention: A Father's Love

There is a study method in the Bible that takes the first use of a word; and normally the word's first use in scripture sets the pattern for its use throughout the Scripture. It is "The Law of First Mention".

The first mention of the word love in the Bible is the love of a father for his son. We hear a lot about mother's love and with good reason; but the first mention of love in the Bible is not of a mother's love for her child, nor of a husband for his wife; but it is of the father's for his son. God says to Abraham in Genesis, *"Take now your son, your only son Isaac, whom you love."* (Genesis 22:2)

One of the greatest love stories in the Bible is found in Luke. Our Lord tells the story of the love of a father's for his son. A certain man had two sons. And the younger of them said to his father, *"Father give me the portion of goods that falls to me."* (Luke 15:12)

So he divided to them his livelihood. And not many days after the younger son gathered all his things together, he journeyed to a far country, and there wasted his possessions with prodigal living. But when he had spent all, there arose a severe famine in that land and he began to be in want. Then he went and joined himself to a citizen of that country who sent him into the fields to feed swine. And he would gladly have filled his stomach with the pods that the swine ate, and no one gave him anything.

But when he came to himself, he said, *"How many of my father's hired servants have bread enough and to spare, and I perish with hunger! I will rise and go to my father, and will say to him, Father, I have sinned against heaven and before you and I am no longer worthy to be called your son. Make me like one of your hired servants."* (Luke 15:18-19) And he arose and came to his father. But when he was still a great way off, his father saw him and had compassion and ran and fell on his son's neck and kissed him. His son then said, *"Father I have sinned against heaven and in your sight and am no longer worthy to be called your son."* (Luke 15:21) But the father instructed his servants, *"Bring out the best robe and put it on him, and put a ring on his hand and sandals on his feet. And bring the fatted calf here and kill it, and let us eat and be merry; for this my son was dead and is alive again; he was lost and is found."* (Luke 15:23) And they began to be merry.

The Love of God

Although this parable of Jesus is often referred to as the "parable of the prodigal son", in it we find the love of a father for his son. The father continued to love his son and accepted him back into his family. This is the last of the three stories that Jesus gave in Luke 15.

In the first story, a man has an hundred sheep. He loses one and leaves the other ninety-nine sheep and goes and searches for the one he has lost until he finds it. He returns home rejoicing and calls upon his friends and neighbors to rejoice with him.

In the second story, Jesus told about a woman who has ten silver coins—the coins of her headdress which was her dowry. She loses one of the coins. She sweeps and searches the entire house until she finds it, and like the shepherd who returns with his lost sheep, she calls her friends and says, *"Rejoice with me, for I have found the piece that I lost."* (Luke 15:9)

We notice that in both these stories; the lost sheep and the lost coin, Jesus said, *"There is joy in the presence of the angels of God over one sinner who repents"* (Luke 15:10).

What do these three stories tell us about the love of God? First, the love of God is committed. People sometimes think that God has turned His back on them and forsaken them. But the shepherd goes after his lost sheep and searches diligently until he finds it. He picks her up. He cradles her in his arms and then joyfully puts her on his shoulders and goes home. Then he calls his friends and neighbors together and says, *"Rejoice with me; I have found my lost sheep."* (Luke 15:6) The woman searches for her one lost coin. She lights a lamp, sweeps the house and searches carefully until she finds it. And when she finds it, she calls her friends and neighbors together and says, *"Rejoice with me; I have found my lost coin."* (Luke 15:9) The father is looking and hoping for the return of his son. He never gives up, never quits, but patiently waits. Notice that he sees the young man, while he is still a great way off. He runs and falls on his son's neck and kisses him. Even though he was undeserving of such love. At the sight of his son, the father runs to him. The son confesses his sin, requesting to be a servant and the father could have ordered this. No doubt that's what his elder brother would have desired. Nobody would have condemned the father for doing so.

The disgraceful son had returned home. He was dirty; he was filthy; a real mess; he smelled like a pigpen. Notice the father didn't ask him to cleanup first before touching him. He had compassion on his son. His older brother however wanted nothing to do with him. He was disgusted with his sinning brother. The attitude of the older brother was the attitude of the Pharisees. "I'm not going to soil my hands by touching this sinner!" But that wasn't the position his father took. He wanted what was best for his son—and nothing but the best. The best was to be a son. The Apostle John said, *"Behold what manner of love the Father has bestowed upon us that we should be called the sons (children) of God!"* (1 Jn. 3:1). We are told in the Word of God, "You belong; You are worthy; You are My child; I am your God." The heart of the father was the heart of God; and Jesus reached out on every occasion to touch sinners. He touched the lepers; He touched the lame; and to heal all who were hurting. Are we prepared to embrace the filthy to heal the hurting? That is the heart of our Father. God reaches out to those He loves, and searches for those who are lost.

What is the first mention of love in the New Testament? In Matthew's Gospel we are told when Jesus was baptized, the voice of God spoke from heaven declaring the love of the Father for the Son, *"This is My beloved Son"* (Matt. 3:17). In Mark's Gospel, the first mention of love was also at the baptism of Jesus where Mark recorded the voice from heaven, saying, *"You are My beloved Son"* (Mk. 1:11). But what is the first mention of love in John's Gospel? *"For God so loved the world that He gave His only begotten Son…"* (Jn. 3:16). God gave His beloved Son. His love for you is unconditional. Furthermore, He desires that you love and be loved by others.

The Love of God

When God created man, He gave to him a will of his own, having the power to choose. He could choose to obey, or to disobey. But whatever his choice, there would be good or bad consequences accordingly. And there would be marvelous benefits if he made the right choice. Adam was crowned with the glory of God and blessed by the love of God with a wife by his side. But they chose to disobey God's one command and brought the awful consequences of their sin upon every generation born thereafter.

Satan entered the garden in the form of a serpent. How this happened, we do not know. But we do know that he hated everything God loved, and was searching for a way to disrupt the plan of God. Seeking to exalt himself above the throne of God, the pride of his heart had caused his banishment from heaven. And here was his opportunity to hurt those whom God loved. He started his subtle deception in the same way he does today. He cast doubt on what God had said to them. He came to Eve first when he said, *"Did God really say....?"* (Gen. 3:1). In his next strategy he appealed to her ego. He told her that she would not die when she ate the forbidden fruit, instead she would simply be like God. So Eve took the fatal bite and gave some to Adam, and he ate. This is called the fall of man, and man has been falling every since.

This is where death began! It was a three-dimensional death:

Instant spiritual death: His spirit died instantly, and for the first time he was separated from God (Ephesians 2:1-5).

Physical death: The separation of body and spirit. His body begins to age and it ultimately dies. (Job 14:1-10).

Eternal death: which the Bible referrers to as the fires of hell. (Matthew 10:28).

All of us one day will answer for how we've lived our lives. If we have lived after the flesh, we will ultimately face death. We must repent of sin and accept Christ as Lord or face that spiritual death which is eternal separation from God.

That is the natural end of a life of sin.

God said to Adam, *"Have you eaten from the tree of which I commanded you that you should not eat?"* (Gen. 3:11)

Few love to hear the sins they love to act.

William Shakespeare

The Blame Game
Then the man said, *"The woman whom You gave to be with me, she gave me of the tree and I eat."* (Gen. 3:12) And every since, man has been passing the blame. A child steals a candy bar: his parents are blamed; the judicial system takes the blame for the crimes committed; the society takes the blame for the murderer. Passing the blame has become the name of the game, and it's as old as man himself.

Not only do we blame one another, but we keep asking the question, "How can a just and loving God allow so much pain and suffering in the world today?" So whether it's natural disasters or man's inhumanity to man, like our forefather Adam, we try to put the blame on God.

A coward is incapable of exhibiting love; It is the prerogative of the brave.

Mahatma Gandhi

But it was the love of God that preached the first gospel message there in the Garden of Eden. God said unto Satan; *"And I will put enmity between you and the woman, and between your seed and her seed; He shall bruise your head, and you shall bruise His heel."* (Gen 3:15)

God's love moved on to put His laws in the hands of Moses. He then engraved them first upon stones, and also upon the hearts of His people. They became the corner stone of all moral law and the basis for man's conscience. The law was our tutor, or as the King James Version says our schoolmaster, to bring us to Christ. Now, we think of the tutor as the teacher. But actually it was the servant who led the child to school where he would learn. So the law is that which God uses to bring us to Jesus Christ so that we might learn how desperately sinful we are, and how hopeless we are to overcome sin. So the law drives us to Jesus Christ.

But the law can't make us righteous; its purpose is to show us our sin in order to make us guilty before God so that we are driven to faith in Jesus Christ. In Acts 15:10, Peter was very honest here. He acknowledged that the Law as it was being taught by the Pharisees was unbearable.

Jesus, Himself was in continual dispute with the Pharisees over the Law. They were constantly accusing Him of violating the Law. Now we know that Jesus did not violate the Law, but He did violate the man-made traditions that grew out of the Law. So Peter said, *"Look, why do we tempt God by putting on their neck a yoke of bondage? Why put this yoke on them? It's been too heavy for us."* (Acts 15:10)

Paul later wrote of the remarkable paradox concerning the Gentiles and the Jews. That Gentiles, who did not pursue righteousness, have attained unto righteousness, even the righteousness which is of faith, but Israel, pursuing the Law of righteousness, has not attained to the Law of righteousness. Why? This is because they did not seek it by faith, but as it were, *"by the works of the Law"* (Rom. 9:30-32) by the law came the knowledge of sin. The Law can only point a finger at you and declare you guilty. But the Law cannot pardon you from your guilt. It can only condemn you. But by faith in Jesus Christ, we have attained unto the righteousness of God. *"There is no condemnation to those who are in Christ Jesus"* (Rom. 8:1).

This is the issue that was splitting the early Church, an issue that is still being faced by the Church today as there are many who will add to the faith the necessity of doing certain works which places people under a yoke of bondage. Rituals cannot save, nor can ordinances. You are saved through faith in Jesus Christ.

Hope For A Troubled Heart

God's law was good, embodied in the Ten Commandments, but man's flesh was weak and unable to keep the law. Therefore God in His unfailing love promised a Redeemer would come. The world needed a Savior who would save His people from their sins. He came on the wings of prophecy, and through the promise of His Word, God sent His Son.

Centuries before Christ came, God planned the political conditions of the earth. Greece was the great world power during the four-hundred-year period before the birth of Christ. God prepared the way for the spreading of His message through Greece by spreading a common language throughout the world. Then the Roman Empire came into the zenith of its power solving the problem of transportation, building a network of roads and developing a system of law and order. So God spread His Word through the early Church by using the common language of the people and the Roman roads and the legal system of that day. The Apostle Paul says, "But when the fullness of time had come, God sent forth His Son..." (Galatians 4:4)

The Son of God became poor that we might become rich. It was love that kept Him on the Cross. One of the soldiers standing by took his spear and pierced His side, blood and water came out. This indicated that Jesus' death was caused by heart rupture; that He died with a broken heart. Surely sin broke His heart, your sins and mine.

> *You may encounter many defeats, but you must not be defeated. In fact, it may be necessary to encounter the defeats, so that you can know who you are, what you can rise from, how you can still come out of it.*
>
> *Maya Angelou*

My dad was a great man of God. He loved to laugh and his laughter was infectious. He had a passion for encouraging others which was very inspiring to me. He founded a little church years ago in Los Angeles, California. After a short while it began to grow and prosper under his leadership. God had blessed us. My sisters and I formed a gospel group. Dad called us the Belfreyairs. Flibby was the lead singer, Faye; the soprano and I, Well I did everything. We sang and shouted; " hallelujah, thank you Jesus" every Sunday morning. The church was thriving, peews were packed, the saints were eager to hear the Word of God.

It's unfortunate, however, when church leaders can't seem to agree without being disagreeable. Nevertheless, dad found himself in the middle of such a dispute. I don't know what happened to cause their disagreement. The Bishop of our jurisdiction said to the pastors under his supervision not to allow a specific Bishop in their pulpits. Quite extreme, don't you think?

Dad was unaware of their dispute. One Sunday evening, when the specific Bishop in question stopped by to congratulate him on the success of his church, dad asked him to have words of expression. Later that evening he received a phone call. It was our jurisdictional Prelate, saying that dad would no longer be the pastor of the church he founded.

Although innocent of any wrongdoing, he lost his church and his dignity as well. He had been a valued minister in the church, but he went home crushed, a broken man, too shocked to know what to do next. But even in the midst of despair, dad found joy in the hope of his salvation. They took his church, but not his laughter. His legacy lives on in the hearts of seven sons, three of whom are ministers of the gospel and three daughters, all of whom are serving the Lord in ministry.

Chapter 7
The Offence of the Cross

By The Shadow of A Cross

In 1967, while training for the Summer Olympics of 1968, as a high diver, Charles Murray, a student at the University of Cincinnati, had special privileges at the university pool facilities. Sometime between 10:30 and 11:00 that evening, he decided to go swimming and practice a few dives. It was a clear night in October and the moon was full and bright. The university pool was housed under a ceiling of glass panes so the moon reflected bright across the top of the wall in the pool area. Charles climbed to the highest platform to take his first dive. At that moment the Spirit of God began to convict him of his sins. All the scripture he had read, all the occasions of his friend witnessing to him about Christ flooded his mind. He stood on the platform backwards to make his dive, spread his arms to gather his balance, looked up to the wall and saw his own shadow caused by the light of the moon. It was the shape of a cross. He could bear the burden of his sins no longer. His heart broke and he sat down on the platform and asked God to forgive him and save him. He trusted Jesus Christ some twenty feet in the air. Suddenly, the lights in the pool area came on. The attendant had come in to check the pool. As Charles looked down from his platform he saw an empty pool which had been drained for repairs. He had almost plummeted to his death, but the Cross had stopped him from disaster.

For the preaching of the Cross is to them that perish foolishness; but unto us which are saved it is the power of God.

1 Corinthians 1:18

Golgotha's Calvary

*At Golgotha's Calvary
there were three who met
One to Remember,
Mercy was she
One to forget,
Justice now satisfied
And One Who bled and died
That Grace might be
To save a wretch like you and me*

Wes Belfrey (1996)

The Cross

It's perched at the top of a chapel. We find it carved into a graveyard headstone, engraved in a ring or suspended on a chain of gold. The Cross is the universal symbol of Christianity. How can a tool of torture come to embody such a movement of hope? The symbols of other faiths are much more optimistic: the six-pointed Star of David, the crescent moon of Islam, and a lotus blossom for Buddhism; but a Cross for Christianity? ... an instrument of execution?

Why is the Cross the symbol of our faith? To find the answer we must look to the Cross itself. Its design couldn't be simpler. One beam is horizontal—the other vertical. One reaches out representing the width of His love; the other reaches up reflecting the height of His love. The Cross is the intersection of death for life. In the death of Christ, God forgave the sinner without lowering His standard of holiness.

The Offence of the Cross

In Philippians, we read of the Apostle Paul's intense desire, *"That I may know Him and the power of His resurrection, and the fellowship of His sufferings, being conformed to His death, if by any means I might attain to the resurrection of the dead."* (Phillipians 3:10)

Many people are looking for a soft religion—an easy ride, nothing but smooth sailing. No suffering, no pain, no trouble, but only sunshine. But the Bible tells us, *"If we suffer with Him, we will reign with Him."* (2 Timothy 2:12) The Bible also speaks of the offense of the Cross referring to Jesus and His death for us on the Cross, and that He is the only way to be saved.

Here is where many are offended. They want the power of resurrection, but they don't want the offense of the Cross. They want the glory without the pain. They want the stars without the scars. They want the riches of His glory, without the sacrifice of His suffering. They say, "I'm willing to receive all the blessings, but spare me having to deny myself and take up my cross to follow Him." I'll take the joy and the laughter, but spare me the humiliation and the scorn. They will turn against you and seek to persecute you.

You now begin to share the sufferings of Christ, who was despised and rejected by man. When Apostle Paul says he wants to know Christ in the *"power of His resurrection,"* (Phillipians 3:10) he does not have in mind eternal life as it pertains to new life in Christ. He is referring to the life every born-again believer experiences in the new birth that is mentioned in Romans 6:4-11.

We are gifted with the ability to hope and to dream, to set goals for our future, and make plans for what we want in life. But what can we do when someone takes our dreams and smashes them into a thousand pieces?

How should we respond in times of crisis or suffering? We can resent suffering, or go through it with joy knowing that our God is in control.

Hope For A Troubled Heart

When Steven of Colona fell into the hands of his assailants, they ask him in derision, *"Where now is your fortress?"* Steven placed his hand over his heart and said, *"Here is my fortress"*.

Sometimes our burdens seem too big for anyone to handle. We are buried in the quicksand of physical and emotional pain. Jesus reaches out with a love that never fails, never forgets, and is always there. Can you hear Him calling, *"Come unto me, all you who are weary and burdened and I will give you rest. Take my yoke upon you and learn from me, for I am gentle and humble in heart, and you will find rest for your souls. For my yoke is easy and my burden is light"* (Matt. 11:28-30). Come! Take! Learn!—such powerful words! We are carrying many burdens. We have the burden to find pleasure, the burden to succeed, the burden to survive, the burden for meaningful relationships—but most of all, we have the burden to know God.

Herein lies an invitation to accept and take advantage of our burdens and our hurts. Our muscles become weak if they are not used. To become strong, a muscle must push against something. To reach the greatest heights, we must learn how to overcome our difficulties.

To Reach For The Greatest Heights,
We Must Turn Our Scars Into Stars

Wes Belfrey (1986)

Comfort and prosperity have never enriched the world as much as adversity has. Out of pain and suffering have come the sweetest melodies of song, the most beloved poems, and the most riveting stories.

There are times in our lives when people say things that wound us. A friend may betray a confidence or spread something that is untrue about us. People who take from us by taking advantage of us cause much of what we go through. Some people are just hard to get along with. In the twenty-third chapter of Acts, we find Paul in prison at a very low

The Offence of the Cross

point in his life. That which he had dreamed of for years to bear witness of Christ before the Jews, had been a disaster. He was rejected by his brethren for whom he had such a deep love and desire to win to Christ. He was discouraged.

So the Lord encouraged Paul. He said, *"Paul, for as you have testified for Me in Jerusalem. It was a total fiasco, but that's alright; you testified. so you must also bear witness at Rome."* (Acts 23:11). So the Lord took him out of the slumps of his past and gave him a call for his future. He set the past aside, reaching for what God had in the future, and it's vital that we do the same. There may be times in your life when you've been forsaken by friends, or even by your own family.

Solomon, who was the wisest man of his time wrote, *"Two are better than one because they have a good return for their work: If one falls down, his friend can help him up. But pity the man who falls and has no one to help him up"* (Eccl. 4:9,10). Hurting people are lonely people. It's as if life is passing you by and nobody seems to care. Loneliness waits in the dorm and hallways of our universities. It lingers around the hospital bed. She is the neighborhood pest, sitting with the wife whose husband spends more time at work than at home.

David Jeremiah wrote, *"What is loneliness?"* Some describe it in physical terms. It's an empty feeling in the pit of one's stomach, almost to the point of nausea. Others describe it as an underlying anxiety—*"a big black pit."* Some say loneliness is a sharp ache in moments of grief or separation. For others, it's *"a long period of stress that wears them down until they're discouraged and defeated."*

The Lord understands your loneliness. Remember that He too was alone in the wilderness forty days being tempted by the devil. Feeling the agony of His impending death on the Cross, once again our Lord finds Himself alone in the Garden of Gethsemane. The word "Gethsemane means "oil press". It is easy to see how it represents those places of deep pressing pain and mental agony.

All of us have our own Gethsemane to endure. It's having a few close friends at those times in our lives that mean the most to us. We lean on them and draw strength from them. Jesus had said to His disciples, *"My soul is exceedingly sorrowful, even unto death. Stay here and watch with Me."* (Matt. 26:38) But instead of watching, they were soon asleep, leaving the Savior to the loneliness of that awful hour of darkness. He prayed, *"O My Father, if it is possible, let this cup pass from Me; nevertheless, not as I will, but as You will"* (Matt. 26:39). If what is possible? —if salvation could by any other way; if man could be saved by any other means—by being good, by being religious, by doing good works, by keeping the Law, by being sincere ... then let this cup pass from Me.

If it were possible for man to be saved by any other way, Jesus would not have gone to the Cross. People sometimes take offence at the Cross. They say it's a bloody religion; But God has shut the world up to the Cross of Christ. It is the only means of salvation. So He agonized in prayer over this cup, until His sweat like great drops of blood fell from His brow. This cup filled was with humiliation, scorn and shame. This cup, filled with His death by crucifixion was set before Him to drink. He was misunderstood, isolated, alone, and betrayed.

Offences may come as a result of living a godly lifestyle, but the believer's lifestyle should be different from that of the secular world.

Peter said, *"If you are insulted because of the name of Christ, you are blessed, for the Spirit of glory and of God rest on you"* (1 Pet. 4:14). When the Bible gives specific commands such as, "Thou shalt not…" then that settles the issue – God need not be consulted. However, where the Bible does not specifically address a particular concern, then we should ask God for His wisdom in what to do under such circumstances.

If we live godly we shall suffer persecution. But let us remember that we are more than conquerors through Christ who loves us. What does it mean to be more than a conqueror? A conqueror is one who goes to war, fights a battle, and wins. To be more than a conqueror is to go into the battle having already won the victory. And that is what we are. Satan has already been defeated. There is no condemnation for us and no way for us to be separated from the love of God. We are victorious in the battle.

The Blood
When we read about blood in the Bible, it means *"a life that has been given."* (Lev. 17:11) Through the blood of His Cross, Christ won the battle once and for all for us.

And you being dead in trespasses and sins and the uncircumcision of your flesh, He has made alive together with Him having forgiven us all trespasses, having wiped out the hand writing of requirements (the Law) that was against us which was contrary to us. And He has taken it out of the way, having nailed it to the Cross, having disarmed principalities and powers, He made a public spectacle of them triumphing over them in it (Col. 2:13-15).

Rejection has to be one of the forms of persecution that hurts the most. As social beings, we have a sociological drive—a need to be needed, accepted, and loved. But all of us have experienced some rejection in our lives. I believe it's hardest when it comes from a member of your own family, or worst yet from your spouse. A soldier while away in Iraq fighting for his country makes a commitment to Christ. When he returns to his home, he may be accused of "foxhole religion" by the ones he loves.

Words are very powerful. They are spirit and carriers of emotions. Words can heal and words can wound. As a matter of fact, some of the most severe wounds are inflicted with words—false accusations, unkind words, words of condemnation, unfair words filled with lies that assassinate one's character. The power of the tongue can be destructive once it is set on fire by hell. The tongue has the power to destroy people. How many people have had their reputations destroyed or their lives made miserable because of someone's tongue? And many times, what is being said isn't true at all.

We need to understand that the power of life and death is in the tongue. We can use our tongues to build up or to tear down. It can infect Christian and non-Christian alike.

When a Christian makes a mistake, he is more predisposed to scandal than someone who is not a Christian. Churches have been torn apart by gossip. Ministries have been destroyed by slander and the indiscretions of a few. May the Lord help us to use our tongues to edify, to encourage, to strengthen, to teach, to comfort, and to give hope!

We may be slandered because of our faith. A university student was verbally assaulted because he wouldn't join his peers on a drinking binge or in a sex party. A woman receives Christ at a church revival. However when she returns home to share her faith, her husband responds by saying, "I don't want a wife who's a Christian." The scripture says it so well, *"They think it strange that you do not plunge with them into the same flood of dissipation, and they heap abuse on you"* (1 Pet. 4:4).

As Christians, we are not exempt from false accusations. However, as believers in Christ, our lives should reflect our confession of faith. Jesus was falsely accused while on trial. The apostles were falsely accused and many of the early church leaders were falsely accused because of their faith. And sometimes we may be falsely accused as well.

But how should we respond? Jesus said, *"Blessed are you when they revile and persecute you, and say all kinds of evil against you falsely for My sake. Rejoice and be exceedingly glad, for great is your reward in heaven..."* (Matt. 5:11,12). However, as Americans, we experience very little suffering in comparison to Christians in other countries. The Bible says that all who want *"to live a godly life in Christ Jesus will be persecuted"* (2 Tim. 3:12).

When people are hurting, we should seek to help them, not add to their pain. And some churches have been accused of shooting their wounded. This may happen when all the blame for the breakup of a marriage is placed on one, instead of both of the spouses. A child goes astray, and it's the parents who are made to feel guilty. A businessman has to file for bankruptcy and people will question his integrity. There are so many ways we can add to someone's hurt. Criticism can weaken and wither the hurting, especially the children who desperately need our guidance and correction. But if we are constantly criticizing them, their spirit will be crused, as well as their ability to succeed.

Dr. James Dobson wrote in his classic, *Dare to Discipline*, "*Too often our parental instruction consists of a million 'don'ts which are jammed down the child's throat. We should spend more time rewarding him for the behavior we do admire, even if our reward is nothing more than a sincere compliment. Remembering the child's need for self-esteem and acceptance, the wise parent can satisfy those important longings while using them to teach valued concepts and behavior.*"

> *In order to console, there is no need to say much. It is enough to listen, to understand, to love.*
>
> Paul Tournier

We should never be too busy to notice the needs of others or too busy to offer a word of encouragement, too busy to drop a note of comfort. An assurance of love can be a healing touch to a wounded heart. We should avail ourselves to care enough to listen when someone needs to talk. Being available should not be a statement we say, but an action we take.

Philip Yancey tells about a man who said nothing when he heard about a family tragedy, and yet spoke volumes. A story is told about Beethoven, a man not known for social grace. Because of his deafness, he found conversation difficult and humiliating. When he heard of the death of a friend's son, Beethoven hurried to the house, overcome with grief. He had no words of comfort to offer. But he saw a piano in the room. For the next half hour he played the piano, pouring out his emotions in the most eloquent way he could. When he finished playing, he left. The friend later remarked, that no one else's visit had meant so much.

It's amazing to me, how easily we can hurt the ones we love. We see examples all around us of the subtle ways in which wives and husbands belittle each other. We never gain in life by hurting others, and a good sense of humor helps us to overlook that which is unpleasant and uncalled for. Sometimes instead of helping those who are hurting, we add to their pain. We should be careful of pointing the finger of blame for the break-up of a marriage at one person only. If people feel safe sharing their problems with us, most likely it's because we are approachable.

The Bible teaches us to be more concerned about the needs of others than our own. We are to encourage and build self-esteem in our relationships to help someone else succeed. We are called upon to have faith, hope and charity: working to treat people the way you would like to be treated; and you will find yourself doing the most amazingly constructive things in this life. But the unbeliever and the fearful will sit in life's parking lot watching life pass him by, afraid to take a chance and never do wonders. How can he? When he's appraising himself and his opportunities on such a low-level basis; he keeps condemning himself. But if such a person will reverse his thinking, and his attitude, about his job, his opportunities, his abilities, about people, and himself, he will begin to achieve his goals.

It's true, some people have succeeded with little or no effort at all; but being blessed is the direct result of what you do. It is God's desire for you to have His blessing, not sin's curse.

At times we do make mistakes—although unintentionally, we offend others. In Psalms, David said, "Who can understand his errors? Cleanse me from secret faults." (Ps 19:12)

David was talking about how miserable he was in Psalm 32:3-5, trying to cover and be in denial about his sins. He finally broke down and confessed his sin, and God forgave him immediately. The Hebrew language indicates that the moment David said, *"I will confess my transgressions unto the Lord,"* (Ps 32:5) God instantly forgave him. If you only knew how willing and ready God is to forgive you, you wouldn't hesitate. Why put yourself through the misery of denial. Don't wait. Receive His forgiveness now. You'll be glad you did.

Years ago, I worked for First Federal National Bank. One day a colleague of mine asked if I could give her a ride home. Her car was in the shop. "Ok, no problem" was my reply. While driving along, I gave her my testimony of how I received Christ as my Savior, and as we pulled up to her home I could see that the Lord was dealing with her heart, as her eyes filled with tears of godly sorrow. So I asked, "Brenda, would you like to receive Christ as your savior?" She replied "Yes." So we prayed a short prayer and by faith she received salvation, calling on the name of the Lord. Because I made myself available, Brenda found Christ, the hope of salvation that day.

Pain: serving on the dark side of Love
At times setbacks are really a blessing in disguise. Paul had many physical sufferings, but he described even greater pressure as he thought on his responsibilities as an apostle. *"I face daily the pressure of my concern for all the churches"* (2 Cor. 11:28). His attitude was not one of failure or self-pity, but one of victory and triumph. Let us go forth with the same attitude. He declared, *"We are hard pressed on every side, but not crushed; perplexed, but not in despair; persecuted, but not abandoned; struck down, but not destroyed"* (2 Cor. 4:8,9). God never sends difficulties into the life of His children without His amazing grace to help in a time of need.

You and I enter this world screaming. Physicians tell us, that one of the first signs of good, healthy lungs in newborns, is that initial, piercing cry. The little angel whose tiny frame has only moments before squeezing its way through a narrow birth canal, screeches in pain when it leaves the warmth of the womb and emerges with a gush into the cold, cruel world—a world of pain. From the time of birth unto the time of our departure out of this life, pain is our often companion, serving on the dark side of love. *"Man that is born of a woman is of few days, and full of trouble"* (Job 14:1).

I heard about courage and hope in the life of David Jacobsen who was a hostage in Beirut for seventeen months. He was head of the largest hospital in West Beirut, when one day in 1985, three men in hoods and wielding machine guns took him captive. Bound and gagged, he was taken from one hideout to another. He spent most of his time on a cold, dirt floor, chained to the wall. Once a day he was fed a tepid, unpalatable mush of watery rice and lentils. As an American, he was hated by his captors. He was just a political pawn and treated cruelly. However, instead of breaking his spirit, he became stronger. He wrote:

> *I discovered that no one's faith was weakened by the hell_ we found ourselves in ___ ... We hostages, with the guidance of Father Jenko, a captive Catholic priest and Rev. Benjamin Weir, who founded the "church of the locked door," a name we chose with some ruthlessness. Grasping hands, we'd quote scriptures and pray. Oddly, our guards seemed to respect this ritual. Our togetherness in prayer showed me that when the Holy Comforter is called, He answers.*

Jacobsen was released in November 1986, but in his final forty-five days of captivity he was alone in a six-by six-by-six cell, his muscles and joints cramped by confinement and the damp aching cold. Yet he said, *"The Presence of God and the Great Comforter, was stronger than ever, especially when I recited Psalms 27 and 102."*

God is the God of all comfort, but we have a responsibility. Paul the Apostle said, *"Praise be to the God and Father of our Lord Jesus Christ, the Father of compassion and the God of all comfort, who comforts us in all our troubles, so that we* can comfort those in any trouble with the comfort we ourselves have received from God" (2 Cor. 1:3,4). We don't really need special titles or credentials in order to be comforters. At some time or another we all are called to the ministry of comfort. *"Therefore comfort each other and edify one another, just as you also are doing"* (1 Thessalonians. 5:11). Speak a word of kindness and share a rose of hope.

Will Not the End Explain

Will not the end explain
The crossed endeavor, earnest purpose foiled,
The strange bewilderment of good work spoiled,
The clinging weariness, the inward strain,
Will not the end explain?
Meanwhile He comforteth
Them that are losing patience. 'Tis His way:
But none can write the words they hear Him say
For men to read, only they know He saith
Sweet words and comforteth.
Not that He doth explain
The mystery that baffleth; but a sense
Husheth a field set thick with golden grain
Wetted in seedling days by many a rain:
The end–it will explain.

Amy Carmichael

One of the reference points of London is the Charing Cross. It is near the geographical center of the city and serves as a navigational tool for those perplexed and confused by the streets.

A little girl was lost in the great city. A policeman found her. In her tears, she explained she didn't know her way home. The officer asked her if she knew her address. She didn't. He asked her phone number, she didn't know that either. But when he asked her what she knew, suddenly her face lit up. "I know the Cross," she said. "Show me the Cross and I can find my way home from there." My friend, so can you. Look to the Cross and you can find your way home. The way of the Cross leads home.

Within the Old City of Jerusalem lies a street in two parts. It has been called the most notorious road in the world, the Via Dolorosa, "The Way of Sorrows," and held to be the path that Jesus walked, carrying His Cross on the way to His crucifixion. According to tradition, it is the route Jesus took from Pilate's interrogation hall to Calvary. The path is marked by stations often used by Christians for their devotions. One station marks the passing of Pilate's verdict; another, the appearance of Simon to carry the Cross.

In all, there are fourteen stations, each one a reminder of the events of Christ's final journey. As to the accuracy of the route, no one knows the exact route Christ followed that day. But we do know where the path actually began. The path began, not in the court of Pilate, but in the halls of heaven. The Son began His journey when He left His home in His search for you and I. The path of the Cross speaks to us of how far God will go to call us back to Him.

Chapter 8
The Hope of Glory

☙❧

Jesus Christ is coming back again. And that promise has been the great hope of every believer down through the ages. One of Winston Churchill's favorite American song was *The Battle Hymn of the Republic*, which begins with the inspiring phrase … *"Mine eyes have seen the glory of the coming of the Lord."* The great creeds of the Church teach that Christ is coming back. The Nicene Creed states that *"He shall come again with glory to judge both the living and the dead."*

There are many variables to the meaning of the word "glory." In one sense, it means "praise and honor given to God" *"And one of them, when he saw that he was healed, returned, and with a loud voice glorified God, and fell down on his face at His feet, giving Him thanks. And he was a Samaritan. So Jesus answered and said, "Were there not ten cleansed? But where are the nine? Were there not any found to return to give glory to God except this foreigner"? And He said to him, "Arise, go your way. Your faith has made you well."* (Luke 17:15-19)

Secondly, "glory" is referred to as *"that which belongs to God"* (1 Cor. 1:26-31). We ascribe "might" unto God because He is the "Almighty God". We ascribe magnificence unto God because He is "The Magnificent One." And we ascribe splendor unto God because He epitomizes splendor and all the attributes of Deity as well (Ex. 16:7).

Sometimes "glory" refers to "heaven" itself, as in 1 Timothy 3:16. When Mahalia Jackson sang of heaven, she sang of glory:

When I Wake Up in Glory

I shall fall asleep someday.
From this earth I'll pass away,
But my soul shall reach up to that land.
When I sing on,
I've cast faith against the host of sin prevail,
I'm gonna wake
We cannot understand

I will wake, wake, wake up yes, in glory.
And with Jesus,
I'll sing redemption story
I shall see His blessed face,
Yes He kept me by His grace
When I wake up,
Yes in glory by and by.

Mahalia Jackson

Apostle Paul urges us in 1 Corinthians, "*Therefore, whether you eat or drink, or whatever you do, do all to the glory of God.*" (1 Cor. 10:31) We were created for the glory of God and it is paramount that we understand this principle. I am to live for the glory of God. That is the purpose of my existence. If we can just do something to the glory of God then we are on solid ground. So the question is, does it bring glory to God? It is foolish to glory in one's self. The only achievements in life that really matter are those done through us by the grace of God for His glory. Every good and perfect gift comes from God and so the glory should go to Him.

The Hope of Glory

You say: "Wes I'm a true success story," when I sing I bring the house down." Well, who gave you such talent? Give Him the credit.

Sometimes glory is hidden from view. Watch the metamorphosis of a cocooned caterpillar as she transforms into the glory of a golden butterfly, or the transformation of a dragonfly in its final shedding stage, as she undergoes a metamorphosis from its nymph form to an adult. The beauty of a red rose has symbolized love and romance for centuries. But her glory is at first hidden from view beneath the earth in a tiny seed.

Hope is an essential part of salvation. Ephesians 2:12 gives us the contrasted condition of the unbeliever: "Before you knew Christ… you were without Christ, being aliens from the commonwealth of Israel, and strangers from the covenants of promise, having no hope and without God in the world.…" Being without Christ, without hope, and without God is the condition of the unsaved. It should never be the condition of the Christian. If we have Christ, then we have hope and we have God. Colossians states, *"To them God willed to make known what are the riches of the glory of this Mystery among the Gentiles: which is Christ in you, the hope of glory." This mystery—the secret of the gospel, which is Christ in you— is the hope of glory."* (Col 1:27)

Christ is our hope. Our only expectation is from Him. Christ in us is our hope of glory. Without Christ in us we have no well-grounded hope of glory. Christ in the gospel; Christ on the Cross; Christ risen; Christ in heaven at the right hand of the Father—all is hope, an everlasting hope to the believer—it's Christ in us: Christ actually present, living, and reigning in us, even as He lives and reigns in glory. This is the only bedrock hope we have and without it we are of all men most miserable. It causes me to focus my life and concentrate my efforts on what's important. And we become effective by being selective. We all at one time or another get distracted by minor issues. We play petty games of inconsequential pursuits with our lives. Many people are like spinning tops, spinning around at a frantic pace, going nowhere fast. Because they have no hope, there's no meaning or purpose to their lives and without a sense of purpose you will keep changing directions, relationships, jobs, careers, churches, moving from one location to another like "a rolling stone gathering no moss," hoping each new change will settle the confusion or fill the emptiness in your heart.

Here, we seem to revert back to subject of ... GLORY

In the Old Testament, no one was permitted to look directly at God (Exodus 19:21,22). Such an encounter would have overwhelmed a person and caused their death. God appeared to His people in indirect ways, ways that revealed His glory to them. God's glory gave the people a taste of what He was all about, while shielding them from the danger of meeting God directly, one-on-one.

So, what is the glory of the Lord? Well, God's glory reflects His uniqueness, and refers to His mighty power, His majesty, and His preeminence. In the Hebrew language the word "glory" is translated weight as in the true weight, or true worth of someone, or something. God's understanding is infinite, and His glory in its fullness is too awesome for words. God's glory is ... God Himself.

The near Eastern countries of ancient times believed in thousands of gods. But the true living God, the Creator of all things, the God of the Bible is like none other.

The Glory of God often took the form of a cloud, or smoke and fire. When Moses went up to Mt. Sinai to receive the Ten Commandments, the top of the mountain was coved by a cloud. And it looked like a fire burning on top of the mountain (Exodus 24:15). The fire represented God's holiness and the cloud, His glory. The cloud represented God's presence with His people. So the purpose of this occurrence was twofold: to reveal, but also to conceal God from view.

Now when Jesus Christ came, He gave us a clearer vision of what the Gory of the Lord is. *"The Word became flesh and dwelt among us and we beheld His glory—the glory that belongs to the only Son of the Father and He was full of grace and truth"* (Jn. 1:14). When He is present, it means God is present. He has the power, the authority, the distinction, and the preeminence. Then to know Jesus is to know God Himself.

Since it's all God's glory, He deserves all of our honor, our reverence, and our worship. This shows us that Jesus is God's glory. Revelation gives us a window into the heavenly worship of Jesus Christ, the kind of worship that He so richly deserves, *"Worthy is the Lamb who was slain, to receive power, and wealth and wisdom, and might, and honor and glory and blessing!" (Revelation 5:12)*

Faded Glory
The Bible also teaches that God gives His people glory—that man made in the image of God reflects His glory. This was man's original state, but due to Adam's fall into sin, the reflection of divine glory became distorted or tarnished. Nevertheless, it is still there and it is God's desire to restore us back into His glorious image.

The Jews had a veil over their eyes from the time of Moses and therefore couldn't see the Lord clearly. But the veil has been lifted for us in Christ, and as we look upon Him—as we behold the glory of Christ Jesus, the Hope of Glory— we are become transformed into the same image from glory to glory, just as by the Spirit of the Lord. The glory faded from Moses' face (the reflection of the glory of the Old Covenant—the Law). It was made weak through the flesh. Moses, the Law-giver, was weak through his own flesh at the waters of Meribah, and failed to sanctify God in the eyes of the people. Instead of speaking to the rock as God commanded, he struck the rock in anger ... crucifying Christ a fresh. As a result, he could see the Promise Land, but could not enter therein *(Deuteronomy 32:48-52)*. But what the Law could not do, grace did when Jesus called him to the mountain top of Olivet.

As aforementioned, when Adam fell, his glory faded. How fleeting is the glory of man. With all of our endeavors to achieve power, glory and wealth, it remains that our only hope of glory is Christ.

In Hebrews we see two very beautiful portraits of hope:

> *Because wanted to make the unchanging nature of his purpose very clear to the heirs of what was promised, he confirmed it with an oath. God did this so that, two unchangeable things in which it was impossible for god to lie, we who have flead to take hold of the hope offered to us maybe greatly encouraged. We have this hope as an anchor for the soul, firm and secure. It enter the inner sanctuary behind the curtain, where Jesus, who went befor us, has entered on our behalf. He has become a high priest forever . . . .*

(Hebrews 6:17-20)

The first portrait of hope here is an altar. e yet. Under the Old Covenant, the altar was a place of protection from the avengers of blood. When you fled to the altar you were safe. The writer of Hebrews says that when all the pressures are against us, flee to the altar, catch hold of the horns of the altar and let nothing pull you away. Why? Because at the altar is hope. (Numbers 35:19)

God's promises are unchangeable and trustworthy because God is unchangeable and trustworthy. When God promised Abraham a son, He took an oath in His own self. The oath was as good as His name, and His name was as good as His divine character and nature.

Jesus said, *"I am the Way, the Truth and the Life. No one comes to the Father, except through Me"* (Jn. 14:6). He embodies all truth, and therefore cannot lie. And because He is truth, you can be secure in His promises; we don't need to worry or wonder if the Lord will change His plans. If we come to Him in faith, believing that He is, He will give us an unconditional promise of acceptance.

The Hope of Glory

Jesus knew that His disciples were heading into some difficult times. Peter would deny Him and feel terrible about it. They would all see Him hanging on the Cross. None of this would make any sense to them. It isn't what they had expected from the Messiah. But Jesus said let not your heart be troubled. But how could they help but be troubled with all they were facing?

The remedy is found in the latter part of this same scripture, "You believe in God, believe also in Me." Jesus was basically saying, "If your heart is troubled, just trust Me." That can be hard to do when times are tough and things don't make any sense to us. But when we go through difficult trials and things don't seem to make sense and our hearts are troubled, that is when we need to hear the voice of Jesus saying, "Trust Me." This assurance should give us courage and hope. By faith I commit my life to Christ, but then I must trust Him to keep that which I have committed to Him.

Sometimes the Lord calms the storm;
Sometimes He lets the storm rage and
calms the child.

Author unknown

The second portrait is an anchor that reaches out of time into eternity, into the very presence of God. In this world we are likened to a small vessel on the sea where everything around us is temporary, unreliable, and subject to change. Nothing here can give us security and stability. But we have an anchor in which both security and stability reside. This anchor reaches beyond the grave—out of time into eternity—and fastens in the Rock of Ages. When we hold fast to hope … this solid hope; we are anchored for eternity. (Numbers 35:19)

When Jesus comes and begins to reign over the earth, we will see the world as God intended it to be. You will not see any one who is disabled. The blind will behold the glory of the Lord! The mute will sing praises unto God and the lame will leap for joy (Is. 35:5,6). There will be no sickness; there will be no more sorrow—the former things will pass away (Rev. 21:4). You will see a world in which people live together in love, in tranquility and harmony—where peace will abide, in a world of righteousness.

Glory

A cloud of gray, came drifting by.
And stopped to say, my name is Mister Gray.
I bring rain, heartache and pain, to the sky of blue.
By cloak and dagger, by mantle of gray,
To hide the light of day.

I am the one, to fade good times away.
My middle name is quite the same,
My middle name is rain,
After a night of shame.
After all, into each life some rain must fall.

They say I'm rude, must I fetch my solitude.
A deep depression, a lover's obsession,
I cause young and old to brood.

Lonely hearts, I'll have a field day.
I socialize in deviled eggs and fine wines of Italy.
I fantasize in cokes cane, her sugar cane,
The word is out, out and about!
I think you better recognize.
Then when in my gin hangover,
They always seem to say,
Hear comes that rainy day,
The party must be over.

The Hope of Glory

Behind you Mister Gray,
The sky is turning black!
Upon the scene, he opened up,
Rumbled proud, rumbled long,
And shouted loud.
I take no prisoners, none at all.
I shook up Nebuchadnezzar, and Rome to fall.
I thunder proud, my middle name is trouble,
Just call me Thunder Cloud.
My depression is severe,
My rain,
Forty days and forty nights,
Of Hugo hurricane.

I am oppression where there is unrest.
I dare not tread, I fly.

They call me cruel, but then again
So is sin.
I'm no fool,
It's man's folly, it's made me strong.
A fool's ideology.

My rod is drawn, now steady, I'm ready.
My romance is a slow dance,
With my cousin crackcousin's crack, or cousin cracked,
Out of the palace, hit the road Jack!
Unto the hog pin of sin,
A drug infested addict's shack,
Leaving death in her wake
And hell at the gate.

Hope For A Troubled Heart

My boast is brash,
My arrow swift in a lane called fast,
I exploit, and trample over
Those cast down, now weak and worn.
Through lust and greed, a desire to succeed

Not gray, not blue, my sky is black.
My middle name is trouble,
I am Thunder Cloud.

Full of Glory on Mt. Sinai,
The Ancient of Days is He.
I am the victory for those in defeat.

Down in the valley, He paws at the gate,
And rejoices in his strength.
My stallion's bold,
My warhorse, strong of old.
I am hope to the weak,
And to them who can't compete.
To whom I am soft and mild.

My Glory is pure, My Majesty,
He who's sure, in judgment, truth,
And liberty.

My pillar is light, to guide the way
In Exodus.
A pillar of fire,
My lamp is righteousness.

In the bosom of the Father,
In eternity past, the Hope of all ages,
The Memrais spelling correct of Scripture, the
Word of the Lord,
The Glory of God,
Full of compassion, the Hope of Glory Am I.

The Hope of Glory

Out of oblivion, I called the atom
Into creation,
Out of the darkness, I called the light,
I called redemption.

Mercy full, I AM that I AM.
The Word born flesh,
The blood of salvation, behold My Glory,
Come unto Me,
All who are weary,
Enter into My rest.

Wes Belfrey (1986)

Chapter 9
Expect a Miracle

❧

Miracle on the Hudson: A Story to Inspire Hope for the Hopeless
"We've had a miracle on 34th Street. I believe now we've had a miracle on the Hudson...", said Gov. David Paterson of New York; as he referred to what has become known as *"the miracle on the Hudson."*

It was less than a minute after takeoff, when suddenly both engines failed. The pilot reported a double bird strike. Dateline NBC aired a report Friday, January 16, 2009, at 10:p.m. by News Travel Contributor, Peter Greenberg, as he explained how fifty-seven-year old, U.S. Airways Pilot and a former fighter jet pilot, Chelsey B. Sullenberger, III. managed to safely land a plane with both engines dead on the Hudson River. US Airways Flight 1549's emergency landing on the Hudson had to be one of the most extraordinary accident sites in the history of aviation. The Hudson, which slices through a famously congested chunk of real estate, was suddenly transformed into a runway paved with water.

What's even more extraordinary is that this time, instead of only looking at what went wrong, air accident investigators will also be studying what went right, as plenty did, beginning with the pilot's actions. *"Pilots around the world were cheering for this guy because we all know what it took to do what he did,"* says Tom Casey, a former pilot of American Airlines, concerning Sullenberger.

According to Casey, Sullenberger did everything he could possibly do in a very short period of time. *"He did it magnificently,"* he adds. In the words of Sullenberger's wife, Lorrie, *"Sully"*, as he is called by his friends, *"is a pilot's pilot."*

Sullenberger and his co-pilot, Jeff Skiles, had a crisis on their hands Thursday. Apparently a flock of birds knocked out both of the Airbus A320's engines. Casey said that while he's experienced bird strikes as a pilot, what Sullenberger and his co-pilot ran into was more like "a flock of bowling balls."

Sullenberger had to think fast. With both engines dead and no power, he quickly realized he was going to have to bring the plane down on the water. Every pilot trains for the ditching, but very few have ever had to pull one off. But that last resort looked like Sullenberger's only resort, as his Airbus Plane lost power and altitude. By all accounts, he pulled it off flawlessly, gliding his Airbus into the water tail first, exactly as the manuals outlined. And that's a major reason the plane didn't break up. "The way he set the plane down, it certainly fell wonderfully nose up—which gave us the shot," said passenger Billy Campbell. But even though the fuselage was sealed before the plane landed, Campbell says the water came into the plane quickly, *"within 20 to 30 seconds, water was up to my knees. And I continued to see it coming in."*

Campbell describes a flight attendant trying to open the back door, but couldn't get it open. This was actually fortunate, because if the door had opened, experts say the plane would have sunk fast. Instead what happened actually turned out to be part of the miracle—the flight attendant began ushering her passengers forward.

Was it luck on the side of the pilot, his crew and his passengers? Or was it a miracle of God? I believe it was nothing short of miraculous. Someone, somewhere, was fervent in prayer for the safe arrival of U.S. Air Flight 1549.

Expect a Miracle

Excepting Miracles along the Way

The shopkeeper was opening a package of merchandise from England. As always he admired the efficient way in which the British packaged things: the sturdy twine, the meticulous care, the careful wrapping.

He noticed a card on top of the contents which read, *"Expect a Miracle."* There was nothing else. He was about to throw the card in the wastebasket, when something stopped him. "What does that mean, 'Expect a Miracle'" he thought. He dropped the card on the counter. But later on when disposing of the wrappings, he noticed it again. *"How come that card was in that package?"* he wondered, *"And who put it there?"*

Was it a mistake? Maybe it fell out of someone's pocket. Or is someone trying to send me a message? He put the card in his shirt pocket and forgot all about it until that night when empting his pockets and he found it again. "Look at this," he said to his wife, 'Expect a Miracle,' "What is that supposed to mean?" The wife being equally puzzled, was a bit more perceptive, "Maybe that is what we need. Our problems seem so overwhelming. Wonder what would happen if we started expecting great things instead of always expecting the worst. Could miracles take place?"

That phrase, "Expect a Miracle," began to get into their thoughts. Like most people, they had problems—one big one and several smaller ones. The next morning the wife said, "What do you say we take that little problem which is bothering us and let's expect a miracle. We have nothing to lose, by testing this 'Expecting a Miracle' business." "You mean some magic?" "I don't know what I mean," she continued. "Maybe we will get some new ideas. Maybe there is a solution. Anyway, what do you say? Let's expect a miracle, really expect it for a few days and see what happens."

And what did happen? Well, the two of them took the first step toward the solution of that little problem by believing it could be solved. But then they went a little farther and believed it would be solved, and that the solution was even then being worked out. And miracles, little miracles started happening. Strange coincidences began developing. All kinds of solutions began coming, one after another–all different. They themselves became different—hopeful, optimistic.

The fact of the matter is that when anyone starts expecting a miracle, he enthusiastically becomes so diligent in faith and hope that he begins to make miracles automatically happen. He finds his way on to the road to miracles. His abilities become focused in a positive way, as opposed to a negative way.

Just One Touch

A woman with an issue of blood was loosing her life. Because of her constant hemorrhaging, she was pronounced unclean by the medical community. Now abandoned by family and friends, she finds herself isolated and alone. She had spent all her money on doctors, but her condition grew steadily worse.

One day she heard about a man who was healing all manner of diseases and giving sight to the blind. Knowing that she must reach him, she set out on her quest for wholeness of life. Out of weakness, she received strength for the journey. By faith she committed, and bursting forth like the dawning of a new day was hope. *"Have you seen Jesus of Nazareth? Have you seen Jesus of Nazareth? I'm looking for Jesus of Nazareth."* Her body is now weakened by the loss of blood, but she continues on. *"What is that I hear, a commotion, a crowd?"* She turns toward the sound and seeing the crowd, began pressing her way. Pushed aside, but she presses on; pushed down, but she presses on. *"If I can just touch the hem of his garment—that's all."*

"If I could just touch Him" Closer, she comes closer to her miracle, and then reaching out, she thrusts herself forward touching with tears of elation, *"Oh! What power! "I feel the power flowing through my body!"* The bleeding stops! She gasps a sigh of relief! Suddenly Jesus stops and turns around, *"Who touched me?"* Feeling the virtue and power flowing

Expect a Miracle

from His body, He knew the touch of faith. Trembling, she comes kneeling before Him. Then came the words which validated her faith. Graciously, He says, *"Daughter be of good cheer, your faith has made you well"* (Matt. 9:22).

A Story of Miracles
One of the definitions for the word "miracle" is "an event which unmistakably involves an immediate and powerful action of God designed to reveal His character or purposes." It is this God-given favor, which I would like to deal with next.

It's a story of miracles, and of the romance of America, land of hopes and dreams. Our story began many years ago in Kansas City. A young fellow with an urge to draw went from newspaper to newspaper trying to sell his cartoons. But each editor coldly, and perhaps a bit cruelly, informed him that he had no talent and advised him to forget it. But the young man couldn't forget his dream. It had a hold on him and wouldn't let him go.

Finally a pastor employed the young fellow for a small fee to draw advertising pictures for church events. But the struggling young artist had to have a "studio," another way of describing a place to sleep as well as to draw. The church had an old mouse-infested garage, and he was told he could stay there. And what do you know? One of those mice became world-famous, as did the young artist. The mouse became known to millions as 'Mickey Mouse,' the artist was none other than Walt Disney.

A wise observation by Demosthenes should be remembered by anyone who wishes to accomplish big things. He said, *"Small opportunities are often the beginnings of great enterprises."* This young man made miracles happen, and on a vast scale, for this once-upon-a-time miracle story grew into motion pictures, which eventuated in Disneyland in California and in Disney World in Florida. And all these marvels happened in America, the land where dreams can come true. If you believe, you can achieve.

Of course, back in those days when he hardly had any money and everyone was giving him the brush off, Walt could have become soured on the establishment walking away a bitter militant like so many today. He just kept believing in his dream and working and making little miracles happen, eventually to become one of the world's greatest masters of childhood fantasy. He reached the heart of America and the people of his country loved him.

There is a law called "The Law of Successful Achievement." It is to have a goal—a sharply focused objective. You must know the will of God for your life. You must know what you want to do and where you want to go, and what you want to be. You must have no doubt about it. The next step is to pray about this goal to be sure it's the right one; because if you acknowledge the Lord in all your ways He will direct your path, and then hold the goal tenaciously in your conscious-mind until it settles down in your heart, for out of the heart pours the issues of life. And when it becomes firmly fixed in your heart you have it, because it has you. Work and keep on working toward your goal. Believe and keep on believing. Pray and keep on praying. Never let up and never give in.

In Wittenberg, Germany, 1517, a young monk marches down the long cobblestoned Collegienstrasse and up to the castle church and nails a piece of parchment to the massive wooden door. The parchment contains his now famous Ninety-Five Theses, written in Latin. Martin Luther, with this document presents an open challenge to the power and practices of the Roman Catholic Church. The brash young cleric is a man on fire, as he sets off one of the greatest upheavals in human history—the Protestant Reformation.

When the Bible says, *"The Kingdom of God is within you,"* (Luke 17: 20-21) it is asserting that God's power and truth are given unto you, and just where in you? Where else but in your heart! Then the principle that all the resources you need are in your heart takes account of spiritual resources. In Ephesians, the scripture clearly states, *"Now to Him who is able to do exceedingly abundantly above all that we ask or think, according to the power that works in us."* (Ephesians 3:20) What power is that, but the power of the Holy Spirit!

And when anyone can be persuaded to think spiritually, to have faith in God, to believe His Word, godly spiritual forces are released on their behalf; the angels of God who hearken to the voice of His Word go to work on situations to bring about good results.

Miracles Out Of a Curse
Some say the catastrophic earthquake that devastated Port-au-Prince, Haiti, January 13, 2010, was because of a pact the Haitians made with the devil some two-hundred years ago. Personally, I don't know, but fifteen days after the earthquake hit, a miracle was discovered buried beneath the rubble of a home near the destroyed St. Gerard University. It was young, seventeen-year-old, Darlene Etienne. She was very dehydrated, with a broken left leg and moments from death when French rescuers pulled her from her coffin of concrete.

"She's alive!" said paramedic Paul Francois-Valette, who accompanied the young survivor to the hospital. The authorities said it is rare for anyone to survive more than 72 hours without water, but here she was fifteen days later. Wow! Darlene's cousin, Jocelyn A. St. Jules, said in a telephone call with the Associated Press, *"We thought she was dead."* But then, two weeks after the earthquake, neighbors heard a faint voice weakly calling from the rubble of a house down the road from the collapsed university building. They called authorities, who brought in the French civil response team. Rescuer Claude Fuilla then walked along the dangerously crumbled roof, heard her voice and saw just a bit of dust-covered black hair down in the rubble. Clearing away debris, Fuilla managed to reach the young girl and much to his amazement she was alive—just barely.

What was it? Who was it that gave her the life-line to keep on breathing, day after day? Was it angels of mercy sent from heaven above? Was it the Mighty Rock of Ages who clefts?

Who covered young Darlene with an angel's wing from crushing blocks and falling debris? May I say ... someone expected a miracle that day!

Deliverance! How to Kick the Habit

In a magazine article entitled *"Back from Happy Town,"* Daniel Negris substantiates these resource principles of *"How to kick the drug habit."* He was a genius at the piano from childhood. He started working with dance bands at fifteen, and in his late teens and early twenties he played with Coleman Hawkins, Henry Jerome, Ben Webster, Red Norvo, Dizzy Gillespie, and the legendary Billie Holliday, who was reputed to be among the best-known jazz musicians in the United States.

Well, one night while hanging out with a saxophonist, an older man, who reached into his shirt pocket and pulled out a long slender cigarette and gave it to Daniel, saying, *"C'mon, man, get with it!"* The boy knew at once that it was marijuana ("pot"). He did not want to show how inexperienced he was, so he took a long drag. Nothing happened at first. Then he began to feel numb from his toes up through his legs and into the upper part of his body. A "roach," or a "blunt duck" is drug paraphernalia in street terms for smoking pot down to it's last drag. Apparently, when you tap a certain level, an insatiable thirst drives you to the point that it's impossible to resist smoking it. He got so he smoked between jobs, smoked in the morning, smoked at night, smoked at all hours.

Then he tried heroin which, he says, has a different affect from smoking "pot." It became so addictive that he was out of control, and he did not care. The other drug addicts assured him that is how it works, so he should "keep cool!" He started arriving late for work and was very high much too often. The bandleader, being disgusted with him, fired him. He lost job after job. While he had not used heroin enough to become a true addict, he had sampled too much, he says, to break free. He realized he needed help, but didn't know where to turn.

Each time Daniel went on a tour his mother put a Bible among his clothes in his suitcase. He never read the Bible—

just let it remain in his bag out of respect for her. Then one night in his hotel room he felt so low that he almost wanted to die. At twenty-three he felt he was through, washed up, finished. And as he sat staring at the blank walls of that cheap hotel room, he thought of the Bible. He took it out of the suitcase and flipped through the pages until finally he saw and read the words of Matthew, *"Come unto me, all you that labor and are heavy laden and I will give you rest."* (Mathew 11:28) Suddenly he jumped up, took his supply of drugs and washed them down the drain. He was now trembling as he fell to his knees, wept and then prayed. Immediately, he says he was filled with Christ's Spirit, felt cleansed and overwhelmed by the love of God. And he writes, *"I have never touched drugs since that night; amazingly enough, my flight from 'happy town' has been total."*

This amazing ability to kick the drug habit in one minute of time dramatically underscores the power of God's Holy Spirit to deliver anyone, anywhere and any time. And when activated by a desperate need, an overwhelming desire and a powerful surge of faith in God, you'll find that He was there all the time.

The Prophet Micah declared, after showing how corrupt the leaders and prophets in Israel were, *"But truly I am full of power by the Spirit of the Lord." (Micah 3:8)*

Jesus told His disciples, "But you shall receive power when the Holy Spirit has come upon you" (Acts 1:8). That is the kind of power Micah was experiencing, and that is the power we also like Daniel need to experience.

How we desperately need the dynamic power of the Spirit in our lives and in our churches. But we have so often substituted other things in the stead thereof. Many of our churches have substituted relevance for His power. They put on the best multimedia presentations and draw people by their drama and entertainment. But they can't really say as Micah said, that he was *"full of the power of the Lord."* (Micah 3:8)

It is a tragic day when a person relies on the gimmicks and the creativity of others to preach the gospel. God has something so much better and so much more powerful for us. It is His Spirit. And we will only minister to the spirits of people by the Spirit of God.

If you can believe, all things are possible to him that believes, and miracles can come true. Just remember, God is not respecter of persons. So when you get discouraged and feel like throwing in the towel, just remember Walt Disney and expect a miracle!

We must be focused and we must have a God-given plan. Additionally, we should surround ourselves with people who are likeminded, those who are optimistic, and those who give wise counsel. Then gather the data, and be willing to reach beyond our comfort zone—that is, outside the box, outside the norm, dare to take a chance. We can't afford to procrastinate, doing nothing ... for indecisiveness can be lethal to success.

Miracles come in all sizes: big ones, medium ones, small ones. And if you start believing in little ones, you can believe in big ones.

Children are a blessing from the Lord. I have three: two daughters and a son. On February 25, 2009, my youngest daughter, Christine, gave birth to twins. And I can honestly say they are two little miracles of joy: Ellis Isaac and Issa Bella. My eldest, Dionne, when pregnant with her first child, Daysiona, the doctors informed her that it would be best to abort the baby because of the high risk danger not only to her health, but to her life. But my wife, Delores, a woman of great faith, strongly objected and said, "Not so! The mother will be fine and the baby as well!" Now that's faith in God—and six months later she gave birth to a darling little angel. It was truly a miracle!

Chapter 10
How to Overcome Feelings of Inferiority

∽∾

I've had people say, "I just don't feel good about myself, or I feel like I can't quite cut it." It's a "can't do" attitude based on a feeling of inferiority. Well, what's the source of these feelings and where do they come from.

Inferiority can be a very destructive force in one's life, like carrying a yoke around on the shoulders all day long. It's emotional baggage that some people carry in their lives and they may not even be aware of it. It becomes a handicap, a determent, an obstacle to what God wants them to become, and to what God wants to achieve in their life.

So if I were to ask you, "Have you ever had any feelings of inferiority?" More than likely some would respond, "I may have." Some would respond with a resounding ... "Yes, yes, yes!" And some would say, "Not only have I had them, but I still struggle with them today."

So let's look for a moment at its source—it's a feeling, a feeling of being less than; feelings like, I'm not good enough, I don't quite measure up, I can't cut the mustard, I'm of poor quality.

It may start in early childhood with name calling or someone putting you down in some fashion. None of us are born feeling inferior; children learn to feel that way. Most

Hope For A Troubled Heart

children learn either from their parents or someone else in those early stages of their childhood.

First, there's verbal criticism. For example, a parent may say, "You were a mistake when I was young and foolish; I didn't want you." Or, "You're not ever going to mount to anything! You're the black sheep of the family!" Names like stupid, dummy, or fatso destroy a child's self-esteem. This fosters feelings of rejection … "I just don't belong."

Then, there are verbal comparisons. A parent may say; "If you were like your brother…" That's devastating to a child. What's instilled in that child is, I know Mom and Dad loves me, but he's the favorite or she's the favorite and he develops an inferiority complex, feeling less than his brother.

Then some parents try to live their lives through their children, so they push them. Sometimes mom pushes her daughter to be a beauty queen because she never made it, or it maybe dad pushing his son to be a football star. So whether by criticism or by comparison, that child learns very early in life to feel inferior. He doesn't become inferior but he feels inferior.

Then again it maybe a physical thing, a physical deformity of some kind, that causes others to stop and stare. It's very evident to everyone—they can't skip or jump, they can't throw a ball, Children at school can at times be very cruel with verbal abuse, especially to a child with a disability. And they feel inferior, "I'm too short, too skinny, a nerd. Or, "She's not pretty at all."

So whatever it stems from, children grow up with verbal criticism and verbal comparisons and situations and conditions in their lives that says you're less than. Sometimes the situation is made worse by physical or sexual abuse, adding insult to injury, where the child is made to feel guilty for the abuse.

A woman who's barren may feel less than her neighbor down the street who has children, or a man who can't seem to compete in the job market, may feel unqualified or incompetent. He's lost his competitive edge since his injury;

How to Overcome Feelings of Inferiority

but his wife is desperate in her endeavor to "keep up with the Jones" next door.

It's a quiet, silent, devastating misery that people live with. It's amazing to me the things people do to maintain a status-level. Status is the world's counterfeit system to reality—I have to look a certain way, drive a certain car, etc. God doesn't judge us according to what other people have. Don't try to live up to the impossible standards that other people set for you to reach.

Now how do these feelings manifest themselves in our lives? Well, sometimes the result is a perfectionist attitude. I want to do everything just right. The perfectionist is often times lazy. "Well I know I could do it today, but I don't feel like it, so I'll wait until tomorrow." And when tomorrow comes it's the same old story. Sometimes you may be feeling fine until something happens or something is said that triggers the incident hidden away deep down in your subconscious mind, and it's as if a dam burst flooding you with tears. So what is the answer? How do I overcome these feelings of inferiority? How do I rid myself of this emotional baggage?

First, we must stop identifying ourselves by someone else's false definition of who we are. How do you see yourself? You are not less than anyone. You were not born to lose, and you can reverse the curse.

There are two extremes of poor eye I-sight. Self-loving; (narcissism) and self-hatred. We have a tendency to swing from one side to the other. One day I'm too high on self and the next day I'm too hard on self. Neither view is correct, as a matter of fact both inaccurate. Where then is the truth?

The answer is in the middle; in between "I can do anything" and "I can't do anything at all" lies *"I can do all things through Christ who strengthens me"* (Phil. 4:13). I am not impotent nor am I omnipotent, not self-sufficient nor insufficient, but Christ-sufficient. It's a self-worth based in our identity as children of God. The Bible says, *"For we are God's workmanship, created in Christ Jesus for good works, which God prepared beforehand that we should walk in them"*

(Eph. 2:10). Notice the word "workmanship." In the Greek language it is translated "masterpiece." That's because you are God's own unique work of art and there will never be another you. Thank God He made you the way you are. Jesus came that we might have life and that we might have it more abundantly. God desires for you to live life to its fullest.

We are either living life to its fullest or merely existing until it's over. Life is to be lived on the highway up to glory, not in the cemetery of broken dreams. Life is not to be lived in the bleachers as only a spectator. But life is an arena, and God's spotlight is shining on you. We must go down into the arena working as co-laborers with Christ. Life is not a parking lot. We have parked too long in idle procrastination. We must move on beyond adversity. We must move on past our setbacks and stumbling blocks, and our fears.

President Calvin Coolidge said:

> *"Press on!—nothing takes the place of persistence; Talent will not, genius will not, persistence and determination alone will win the day!"*
>
> *Calvin Coolidge*

Helen Keller was blind, deaf, and dumb, but moved on to inspire the world with being an academic genius. She wrote the best and most wonderful things in the world cannot be seen or touched, but just felt in the heart. The incredible story of her life inspired a major motion picture entitled *The Miracle Worker*.

Severe depression knows no mercy. Beethoven once sat in the seat of depression and deafness, but moved on to write some of the most beautiful music the world has ever known.

Abraham Lincoln pressed on past the pain of lost love, beyond the pain of a nervous breakdown, and overcame the frustration of eleven consecutive political defeats to become the President of the United States. Whatever you've gone through, it's not as important as what you're going to.

How to Overcome Feelings of Inferiority

The Attitude of Altitude

J. Cid Low Baxter said, *"What's the difference between an obstacle and opportunity? The answer is our attitude towards it."*

When Jeff Steinberg appeared onstage, the audience seemed to gasp. His body tragically distorted, and it was difficult for him to walk. His head was disproportionately large for his body, and he held a microphone with the hooks he used for hands. But his smile was bigger than his disability. Jeff had a song and a slogan that was uniquely his ... *"I'm a masterpiece in progress."*

Instead of focusing on his physical problems, he looked at the gifts God had given him and used them fully. He could laugh, he could sing, and he could tell about God's love.

We all have problems that we face every day, and ultimately it's our attitude that counts—attitude toward ourselves and toward God. Attitude is the "advance man" of our true selves. It is how I react in the face of criticism. Your attitude determines your quality of life. Life can be likened to a grindstone. Whether it grinds you down or polishes you, depends on what you are made of. Fire melts clay, but hardens steel, transforming it into permanency, and also purifies gold.

If what you're doing doesn't have resistance, it's not worth doing. Without the resistance of water ships can't float, and without the resistance of air planes can't fly. Rubber is nothing until you stretch it, so stretch your faith in God. And should things get tough as the battle heats up, remember the tea kettle ... though it's up to its neck in hot water, it keeps on singing!

Albert Einstein is considered to be one of the world's greatest scientific geniuses. Winner of the Nobel Prize in Physics in 1905, he is credited with the Theory of Relativity. But did you know, Einstein was expelled from high school. As a matter of fact, at age nine, he was still unable to speak fluently and was told by one of his teachers that he would never amount to anything. He was actually expelled from school because he was "so slow." What would have happened if young Einstein had allowed that teacher's thoughtless opinion define who he was?

Nathaniel Hawthorne came home heartbroken. He'd just been fired from his job in the House of Customs. But his wife, rather than responding with anxiety, surprised him with joy. *"Now you can write your book!"* "And what shall we live on while I'm writing it?" he asked. To his amazement she opened a drawer and revealed a bundle of money she'd saved out of her housekeeping budget. *"I always knew you were a man of genius,"* she told him. *"I always knew you'd write a masterpiece."*

Ladies, she believed in her husband. And because she did, he wrote. And because he wrote, every library in America has a copy of The Scarlet Letter by Nathaniel Hawthorne. My friend, you have the power to change someone's life simply by the words that you speak. *"Death and life are in the power of the tongue"* (Prov. 18:21).

Emily Dickinson is said to be one of the most beloved of all American female poets. She wrote over seventeen hundred poems. In one of her most famous poems, *"Hope is the Thing with Feathers,"* she equates hope with an imagined bird that lives in the soul:

> *"Hope" is the thing with feathers -*
> *That perches in the soul -*
> *And sings the tune without the words -*
> *And never stops - at all -*
>
> *And sweetest - in the Gale - is heard -*
> *And sore must be the storm -*
> *That could abash the little Bird*
> *That kept so many warm -*

How to Overcome Feelings of Inferiority

I've heard it in the chillest land -
And on the strangest Sea -
Yet - never - in Extremity,
It asked a crumb - of me.

Emily Dickinson

Ever hear the parable about the eagle which thought it was a chicken? One day, so the story goes, an adventurous young boy climbed high in the mountains near his father's chicken-farm and found an eagle's nest. He took an egg out of the nest, brought it back to the farm and put it with the chicken eggs underneath a setting hen. The hen sat on the eggs until they hatched and out came a little eaglet along with the chicks. The eaglet was raised among the chickens and never knew it was anything else but a chicken. For a while it was content and lived a normal chicken's life.

But as it began to grow, there were strange stirrings within. Every once in a while it would think, "There must be more to me than a chicken!" But it never did anything about it until one day a tremendous eagle flew over the chicken yard. The eaglet felt strange new strength in its wings. It became aware of an enormous heartbeat in its breast. And as it watched the eagle, the thought came, "I'm like that. A chicken-yard is not for me. I want to soar across the sky and perch on mountain peaks." It had never flown, but the power and instinct were within. It spread its wings and was lifted to the top a low hill and finally on into the blue to the crest of a high mountain peak. It had discovered its great self. Remember that nobody can be you as well as you can. But you must discover who you are in Christ.

A leaf blows in the wind, but an eagle rises against the wind. Although the winds of recession are blowing across our nation, somewhere, an eagle is rising against the wind. The choice is yours! Are you a leaf blown in the wind, ever downward, ever falling, caught in the winds of change, or as a believer in Christ, an eagle rising against the wind!

Which one are you? A "How" Thinker, or an "If" Thinker"

What is the important distinction between an "if" thinker and a "how" thinker. The "if" thinker will worry over a difficulty or a problem, thinking to himself: If only I had done this or that; If the circumstances had been different; If others had not been so unfair to me. So he goes from one weak rationalization to another, round after round, getting nowhere. You don't need to be one of those defeated "if" thinkers.

But, the "how thinker" wastes no energy on post-mortems when trouble hits. He immediately looks for the best solution, knowing there is always a God-given solution. He asks himself, "How can I work something good out of this? How can I make a comeback?"—not "if," but "how."

The "how thinker" is a "hope thinker". And since *faith is the substance of things hoped for, the evidence of things not seen,"* the "how thinker" is a faith believer (Heb. 11:1). The "how thinker" gets problems solved because he knows values are to be found in difficulties. You must eliminate destructive thinking and replace it with constructive thinking. And waste none of your time with the futile 'if's' but go right to work on the creative 'how's'. And never—I say never, give up!

There are three 'how's' in getting on top of things: (1) is the "try—really try" principle, (2) "believe—really believe," and (3) "pray—really pray." When taken together, they cancel out the futile "doubt's" and "if's" and underscore the creative "how's".

When God created man, He put a touch of greatness into his nature. Man is a paradox—on the one hand there's goodness and faith, and on the other there's futility and sin; he's a mixture. But however weak, mixed up, however defeated he can be, there is still this element ... something in him entitles him to become and to be called a child of God. No matter what has happened to him in the way of difficulty and trouble, he still has the resilience to come out of it with dignity and power.

How to Overcome Feelings of Inferiority

Develop a "can do" attitude as the Apostle Paul when he declared, *"I can do all things through Christ who strengthens me."* (Phi. 4:13) Men and women who never knew what they couldn't do have accomplished some of the greatest things in this world. So, not knowing they just went right ahead and did it.

A good example of this was Tom Dempsey, who kicked that unbelievable sixty-three-yard field goal that electrified the athletic world some years ago. Tom was born with only half a right foot and a deformed right hand. He had some really great parents, for never once did they make him uncomfortably aware of his handicap. As a result, the boy did everything everybody else did. If the Scouts hiked ten miles, so did Tom. Why not? There was nothing wrong with him. He could do it the same as any other kid.

Then he wanted to play football, and of all things, he got the desire to excel in this special talent. He found he could kick a football farther than anybody with whom he played. To capitalize on that ability he had a special shoe designed. With never a negative thought about that half right foot and deformed right hand, he showed up at a kicking try-out camp and was given a contract with the Chargers. The coach, as gently as he could say it, gave him the word that he didn't have what it takes to make it in pro football, and to try something else.

Finally, he applied to the New Orleans Saints and was given a chance. The coach was doubtful, but impressed by the boy's belief in himself, so took him on. Two weeks later the coach was even more impressed when Tom kicked a fifty-five-yard field goal in an exhibition game. That got him the job of regular for the Saints, and in that season he scored 99 points for his team.

Then came the big moment. The stadium was packed with 66,000 fans. The ball was on the twenty-eight-yard line, with only a few seconds to play. The play advanced the ball to the forty-five-yard line. Now there was time for only one play. *"Go in there and kick it Dempsey,"* the coach shouted.

Hope For A Troubled Heart

As Tom ran onto the field he knew his team was fifty-five yards from the goal line, or sixty-three yards from the point at which he would have to kick. (The longest kick ever in a regular game had been fifty-five yards by Bert Rechichar of the Baltimore Colts.) The snap of the ball was perfect. Dempsey put his foot into the ball squarely. It went straight, but would it be far enough? The 66,000 spectators watched breathlessly. Then the official in the end zone raised his hands, signaling it was good. The ball had cleared the bar by inches. The team won, 19-17. The fans went wild, thrilled by the longest field goal ever kicked, and by a player with half a foot and a deformed hand!

Unbelievable!" someone shouted. But Dempsey smiled. He remembered his parents. They had always told him what he could do, not what he couldn't do. He accomplished this tremendous feat because, as he so well put it, *"They never told me I couldn't."*

Never tell yourself that you can't do this or that; never assert doubt that it just isn't possible. Only tell yourself that I can do all things through Christ who strengthens me. Remember that chicken-eagle story? Be the eagle that you really are!

Charles F. Kettering, the great inventive genius, once remarked, *"I am not interested in the past. I am interested only in the future, for that is where I expect to spend the rest of my life."* And remember, that future where you are to spend the rest of your life is determined by your attitude. You'll find all the resources for it in the power that works mightily in you.

Chapter 11
The Dark Side of Love

☙❧

Hebrews states, *"And you have forgotten the exhortation, which speaks to you as sons: My son, do not despise the chastening of the LORD, nor be discouraged when you are rebuked by Him; for whom the LORD loves He chastens, and scourges every son whom He receives."* (Hebrews 12:5-6)

It is important for us to understand that although God chastens us, it is because He loves us. The chastening of the Lord is never punitive, but is always corrective. God doesn't punish us; He corrects us. There is a difference between correction and punishment.

We, as parents know how important it is to correct our children. If you see your child running out into the street without looking, you realize the danger that he's in and you correct him. Our heavenly Father sees us doing things that can destroy us and He corrects us. It's for our benefit, for our own good, that He does so. It may be painful, but not as painful if He allowed us to continue along our destructive path. It's better to suffer the pain of chastisement now, than to suffer the pain of eternal judgment later.

When you feel that you're being disciplined by the Lord, don't resist it or resent Him for it. Understand it as evidence that you are His child, and that He loves you very much.

I've had mothers ask me to pray that God would save their children. One little grandmother came up to me on a Sunday after service. With tears in her eyes, she was asking for prayer that God would save her grandson.

The book of Zephaniah presents an aspect of God's love that could be called the dark side of love. How could love be the theme of this book seeing it is a book of judgment? Well to illustrate this I'd like to tell you a story. It's a mystery story. It's a story to help us understand the dark side of God's love.

It was late at night in a suburban area, of one of our great metropolitan cities of America. A child lies restless in bed, a man with a very severe and stern look enters her bedroom and he softly approached her bed. And the moment the little girl saw him, a look of terror came over her face and she began to scream. Her mother rushed into the room and went over to her as the trembling child threw her arms about her. But the man withdrew to the telephone and he called someone who was evidently an accomplice and in a very soft voice made some sort of an arrangement. Then hastily the man re-entered the room; He tore the child from her mother's arms and rushed out to a waiting car. The child was crying and he attempted to stifle her cries. He drove like a mad man, down street after street until he finally pulled up in front of a large sinister looking building. All was quiet.

The building was partially dark, but there was one room upstairs ablaze with light. And the child was rushed inside up to the lighted room and put into the hands of the man waiting in the hallway with whom he had the phone conversation with. In turn the child was handed over to another accomplish, and this time it was a woman and these two took her into an inner-room and the man who had brought her was left outside in the hallway. Inside the room the man that took her in there took a long sharp knife and plunged it into the vitals of that little child's body. She lay there in silence, as if she were dead.

Now what is your reaction at this point? Maybe you're saying, "I certainly hope someone catches that crook that abducted that little child and is responsible for such an awful crime."

The Dark Side of Love

But I have not described to you the depraved and degraded action of a debased mind. It is not the sorted and sadistic crime of a psychopath. This is not a murder mystery story. But on the contrary I have just described to you a tender act of love. As a matter of fact I know not of a more sincere demonstration of love than I've described to you in this story.

Now let me fill in the blanks so that you'll understand.

That little girl had awakened in the night with severe abdominal pains. She had been subject to such attacks, so as instructed by her doctor, her parents were watching her very carefully. And it was actually her father who had rushed into the room. The little girl knew that she might have to make that trip to the hospital and when the father rushed into the room she screamed of course. And he talked to the specialist about it and when he saw the suffering of his little girl, he went to the telephone and called the family physician, making arrangements to meet him at the hospital. So he rushed his own little girl down to the hospital. There he handed her over to the family physician and the doctor had taken her into the operating room with the nurse where he performed an emergency surgery. Through it all, every move and every action of the father was of anxious care and tender love ... the dark side of love. But love nevertheless.

Now the father loved that child just as much on that dark night when he took her to the hospital and delivered her to the surgeon's knife as he did the next week when he brought her flowers and candy. It was just as much a demonstration of deep affection, when he delivered her into the hands of the surgeon, as it was the next week when he brought her home and delivered her into the arms of her mother.

Love places the eternal security and welfare of the object of love above any transitory or temporary comfort or present pleasure here on this earth. In fact, love seeks the best interest of the beloved. That's what the book of Zephaniah is all about—the dark side of love.

Hope For A Troubled Heart

In our society today many of us have come to the place where the love of God is exaggerated out of proportion to the other attributes of our God. His love has been presented in such a way where it appears to be a weakness rather than a strength. There is the sunny side of the street, with nothing of the other side ever mentioned. There is a love of God that's presented that sounds more like a fun time with grandma and grandpa, rather than the vital concern of parents for the welfare of their child.

God deals with us according to our need in the dark side of love. The Great Physician will put His child on the operating table and He'll use the surgeon's knife to cut out the tumor of transgression, or a deadly virus sapping our spiritual life, or when He sees the cancerous growth of sin. He does not hesitate to operate. Cutting deep, He makes His incision, with the Sword of His Spirit; it is living and powerful, sharper than any surgeon's knife, sharper than any two-edged sword, piercing even to the division of soul and spirit, and of joints and marrow and with x-ray vision, it is a discerner of even the thoughts and intents of the heart.

Isaiah, under the inspiration of the Holy Spirit, wrote of the promised Messiah—the One who understands the dark side of love more than any other is—the Man of Sorrows. The prophet wrote the original script concerning Christ's sufferings long before Mel Gibson ever thought about making a motion picture that would dramatically focus on His sufferings.

We really don't think of the Messiah in terms of weakness, deep sorrow, and grief. The disciples, when they walked with Jesus, thought He would conquer the Romans and restore the kingdom to Israel. Yet Isaiah describes Him as a *Man of Sorrows and acquainted with grief.*

Read the prophet's heart-wrenching prophecy from Chapter 53:

> *He was despised and rejected of men, a man of sorrows, and acquainted with grief; and like one*

> *from whom men hide their face. He was despised, and we did not esteem Him. Surely our griefs He Himself bore, and our sorrows He carried; yet we ourselves esteemed Him stricken, smitten of God, and afflicted. But He was pierced through for our transgressions, He was crushed for our iniquities; the chastening for our well-being fell upon Him, and by His scourging we are healed (Isaiah v. 3-5). He was oppressed and He was afflicted, yet He did not open His mouth; Like a lamb that is led to the slaughter, and like a sheep that is silent before its shears, so He did not open His mouth (v. 7). But the Lord was pleased to crush Him, putting Him to grief... As a result of the anguish of His soul, He will see it and be satisfied by His knowledge of the Righteous One, My Servant will justify many, as He will bear their iniquities (v. 10-11).*

Through this passage we understand that Jesus endured, and therefore He understands the depth of human pain and suffering. Let's look again at the words of Isaiah: despised, crushed, oppressed, afflicted, scourged, pierced, smitten, stricken, like a lamb led to slaughter. Yes, He's been there and it was for us that He tasted death. We would rather think of the Messiah as winning, as opposed to losing. As the disciples who walked with Him, we also want to see Him in His glory coming on a white horse. We like Him to be conquering and triumphant. But that is not the way He was predicted to be in His first coming.

Hebrews states this theme of Christ's suffering, *"Who In the days of His flesh, He offered up both prayers and supplications with loud crying and tears to the One able to save Him from death, and He was heard because of His piety"* (Heb. 5:7). Isn't that something! The Son of God, in all of His deity, being also fully human, felt the sting of impending death and called on His Father for comfort and help in the dark side of love.

Pain and suffering—words from which we try desperately to escape. But Jesus accepted the pain; He endured it, and embraced it. Webster's Dictionary defines "physical pain" as *"a basic bodily sensation induced by a noxious stimulus, received by naked nerve endings, characterized by physical discomfort...acute mental or emotional distress."*

Jesus knew such physical and emotion pain. Being the "Man of Sorrows" that He was, He understands and identifies with our deepest hurts and struggles.

Phillip Yancey, in his insightful work, "Where is God When it Hurts":

> *I have never read a poem extolling the virtues of pain, nor seen a statue erected in its honor, nor heard a hymn dedicated to it. Pain is usually defined as 'unpleasant-ness.' Christians don't really know how to interpret pain. If you pinned them against the wall, in a dark, secret moment, many Christians would probably admit that pain was God's one mistake. He really should have worked a little harder and invented a better way of coping with the world's dangers. I am convinced that pain gets a bad press. Perhaps we should see statues, hymns, and poems to pain. Why do I think that? Because up close, under a microscope, the pain network is seen in an entirely different light. It is perhaps the paragon of creative genius.*

Emotional or mental pain is not quite as objective. C. S. Lewis adds this comment ... *"Mental pain is less dramatic than physical pain, but it is more common and also more hard to bear. It is easier to say 'My tooth is aching' than to say 'My heart is broken'...."* In other words, it's hard enough to go to a dentist when I have a bad tooth, but where do I go with this broken heart of mine? Where do I go when the pain seems unending, the effect of which can be devastating? The answer is not difficult: We can go to the Man of Sorrows, Who is acquainted with grief, who understands our brokenness and pain. Suffering has a way of turning us around, back to the Lord which proves essential for our spiritual growth.

The Prophet Jonah was called by God to go and preach to the Assyrians in their capital city of Nineveh. But the last thing Jonah wanted to do was to preach to these evil Assyrians. He wouldn't want to associate with them, and he surely wouldn't want to be successful and see them spared of God's wrath.

As the story unfolds, we learn much about God. We see His sovereignty as Jonah learns that if God is taking you to Nineveh, then that's where you are going. Take a boat or take a fish, the hard way or the easy way ... God will accomplish His purposes. We also see God's love for the Gentiles. God didn't want to destroy the Gentiles; He wanted them to be saved. God's heart was moved with compassion even toward the most evil of Gentiles. We also see the grace of God toward Jonah and Nineveh.

Finally the story provides a beautiful picture of the Resurrection of Jesus Christ, as Jesus Himself pointed out. The men on the ship didn't want to throw Jonah overboard. They rowed hard and tried everything they could, but he insisted that they needed to throw him over. Jonah thought that he would drown, but that the ship and her crew would be saved. And at this point, he would rather die than go to Nineveh.

I think it's both amazing and sad the kind of men God has to use to accomplish His purposes. A man who would prefer death to obeying God, and yet God used him to bring about a major revival in a mighty, but evil city. It is actually amazing that God uses any of us, but isn't it wonderful that He does. And the fact that He uses people like Jonah and people like us just makes all the more miraculous and more obvious that it is He and not us.

After being in the belly of the fish for three days and three nights, Jonah finally prayed. What took him so long? So often it takes God time to break the people He wants to use. At times we are so stubborn. We want to do it our way, not His.

God knows that we can never attain the full potential of our ministry until we've been broken. It's when we've been tried in the fire that we come forth as pure gold. The experiences that pressure us and break us are some of the healthiest experiences of our lives. They cause us to cry out to Him.

Let's look for a moment at Jonah's cry: Then Jonah prayed to the Lord his God from the fish's belly. And he said:

> *I cried out to the Lord because of my affliction, and He answered me. Out of the belly of hell I cried, and You heard my voice. For You cast me into the deep, into the heart of the seas, and the floods surrounded me; all your billows and Your waves passed over me. Then I said, 'I have been cast out of Your sight; Yet I will look again toward Your holy temple.' The waters surrounded me, even to my soul; the deep closed around me; weeds were wrapped around my head. I went down to the moorings of the mountains; the earth with its bars closed behind me forever; yet You have brought up my life from the pit, O Lord my God. When my soul fainted within me, I remembered the Lord; and my prayer went up to You, into Your holy temple.*

(Jon. 2:1-7)

For Jonah, there was no light of the day, only the darkness of night as he journeyed on the dark side of love. Thankfully, Jonah's prayer was heard and God spoke to the fish to deliver him on dry land again. And although the city was a three-days journey away, Jonah made it there in one day. You'd think he learned his lesson?

Jonah's message was a simple one: "Yet forty days, and Nineveh shall be overthrown!" (Jonah 3:4) He gave them no exception, not even an opportunity to repent. His message sounded like judgment was imminent.

But the whole city, including the king, repented in sackcloth and ashes. They thought, *"Who can tell if God may turn and relent, and turn away from His fierce anger so that we may not perish?"* (Jonah 3:9) They were given no chance of forgiveness, but still they repented. They thought there just might be a chance for them.

By comparison, we today have God's promises of forgiveness, if we confess our sins, and yet we often fail to repent. This is why Jesus said the men of Nineveh would testify against His generation (Matt. 12:41). All the Ninevites had was a word of condemnation, and yet they repented. We have a promise of forgiveness through Christ, and yet we resist Him.

Now what was God's instrument of correction in this story?—a fish that He prepared to discipline Jonah.

There are men who reject the legitimacy of this story; they say it's impossible that God would make a fish that could keep a man alive inside for three days. Yet, we take for granted the fact that man can make a vessel that can take people under the sea for weeks and return them safely to dock. If man can do it, surely God can. Oh, how little we understand about the power of God!—if we think that He can't accomplish at a minimum that which man can do when He is the one Who created him. Our God created every living being that has ever walked, crawled, or crept on the face of the earth; flown through the air; or swam the depths of the sea. Is this anything in comparison? Of course not! He is able to do exceedingly abundantly above all we ask or think about.

What is God's instrument of correction for you and I when we are wrong? It is the rod of His word, the sword of His Spirit.

David was a man after God's own heart, but in 1 Samuel he fell into a backslidden condition on the dark side of fear and unbelief. Here, he sinks to his lowest as his backsliding hits rock bottom. He was preparing to go to war against Israel, which in essence meant against God. It was then that he made this shocking statement: *"That I may not go and fight against the enemies of my lord the king."* (1Samuel 29:8) David was calling Achish his lord and the people of God, his enemies.

When we begin to backslide, we never think that we will sink as low as we sometimes do. Here again is proof that God uses ordinary people, subject to failure, men of like passions, to accomplish His purposes. But while David was in the enemies camp, walking in the valley of darkness, sowing to the wind, he was about to reap the whirlwind. The Amalekites invaded the city of Ziklag, burned it with fire, and took their wives and children captive.

David had been through a rough time of backsliding. He had done many things of which he was ashamed. And now he was even rejected by the Philistines. His own little band of men was turning on him with contemplation of stoning him. Faced with the tragedy of loosing their families, David's men began to turn against him and even talked about killing him. They looked for someone to blame, rather than planning a rescue.

The good thing about all this is that David hit bottom. And when he hit bottom, he looked up. Sometimes God will allow His people to hit rock bottom, if that's what it will take to bring them to their senses. Sometimes we have to go down before we can rise up. We may have to go down to the "woodshed" of God's chastening before we repent and look up. And if we are depending on anything other than God, He will remove those things we are trusting in, so that we will have no place to turn but to Him. It is much easier to just turn to Him willingly, if you are in a backslidden state; but He will wait until you hit bottom, if that's what it takes.

Well, David did look up and strengthened himself in the Lord his God. He turned to God for strength. He had no one else, so he turned back to God. He then inquired of the Lord and received guidance from Him. But David took strength from the Lord, and he began looking for a solution instead of a scapegoat.

When we are troubled and facing problems, it is useless to look for someone to blame. Instead of looking for a scapegoat, earnestly consult God as to how you may assist with the solution. David asked God for His help, "Shall I pursue this troop? Shall I over take them?" And God answered him, "Pursue, for you shall surely overtake them, and without fail, recover all." Scattered over the countryside, there the Amalekites were ... eating, drinking and reveling because of the great amount of plunder they had taken from the land of the Philistines and from Judah. But David attacked them from the twilight until the evening of the next day; he rescued his wives, and nothing of theirs was lacking—neither small nor great, neither sons nor daughters, nor anything which the Amalekites had taken from them; he recovered all. Why? Because he trusted the Lord is God.

Jesus our Lord experienced the dark side of love for you and I. And in spite of the fact that He knew all His life He would suffer a horrible death on the Cross, such knowledge did not remove the internal agony He endured when that awful hour arrived. He knew for thirty-three years that the cup of suffering would come. But knowing all of that for so long, did not alleviate nor cancel the emotional and psychological pains of His impending death. Indeed, the full weight of His sufferings fell upon Him at Gethsemane as He pleaded for relief.

Here lies a vital lesson for all of us: we are never more presumptuous than when we try to give hurting people what feeling we think they ought to have in their time of anguish. How could we dare invade that tender emotional space? Now there are occasions when another's anguish can be essential for the accomplish-ment of God's plan, but even though some of us wish to rescue others from their own Gethsemane, we need to restrain ourselves from doing so. Let's guard against cutting in on God's plan for their lives. You can't fix how people feel; our best involvement should be to: be available, stay near and be silent, and to keep watch and pray. Just stay near and be silent. Be available with your support. Jesus understands better than any of us, the silent cries from the dark side of love.

The brutality of the Cross was horrific like none ever experienced by anyone before, nor since. A quick glance at Matthew's account provides us with an overview of the intensity of what Christ endured physically. First, He was seized and treated harshly like a common criminal. They spat on His face, He was slapped, and He was beaten beyond recognition. He was bound and scourged according to the gospel writers (Mark 15:15); He was spat on again and beaten with a reed (Matt. 27:30). He was crucified as they drove spikes into His hands and feet; later a sword was thrust into His side (Matt. 27:35, Jn. 19:37).

Can you imagine the horror of having iron spikes pounded into your hands and feet? No wonder the songwriter said, *"Can't you hear the hammer ringing; can't you feel 'O' death a stinging."* Imagine the excruciating humiliation of being hung naked and in plain view for everyone to see your shame. It must have been a deplorable sight. A horrible event to witness, to say nothing of personally enduring it! The body of Jesus had been so mutilated that he didn't even look human. We can't even imagine the physical suffering He must have borne; it is nothing short of mind-boggling. But still there was another side to this darkness that He felt and endured—a pain more severe than that which He felt physically. Yes, the physical pain of Jesus was horribly intense, but the agony of being separated from His Father goes much farther/further than our ability to imagine. Matthew writes, *"Now from the sixth hour, darkness fell upon all the land until the ninth hour. About the ninth hour Jesus cried out with a loud voice", saying, 'Eli, Eli, Lama, Sabachthani?' That is, 'My God, My God why have you forsaken me?"* (Matt. 27:45,46). For the first time in eternity, God turned His back on His Son.

At that moment that Christ took on all our sins. He bore on the Cross our transgressions, as He took our guilt, our condemnation and our hell. That is why the Father could not look on Him. He had become sin for us. Jesus experienced the ultimate darkness—the sting of death and separation from God, His Father. But thank God because of Christ's shed blood, it is a pain that you and I will never know.

In absolute loneliness and in the weakness of crucifixion, He cried out, "Why have You forsaken Me?" I want to assure you that there is no way you can have a heartache that Jesus does not understand, nor one with which he cannot identify. No physical pain that you endure escapes His awareness—no disability nor grief, no heart-attack, no fear—regardless of how debilitating—that Christ cannot understand or feel; for He has felt it all in the dark side of love. Therefore, know for sure that He's there to walk with you through the valley of the shadow of death and if you allow Him as David did, you'll find His rod and His staff to comfort you there.

The Accusers, the Accusation, and the Adulteress
This has to be one of the most and heart-rending scenes in the entire Bible…

The stage is set, the curtain rises, and there in the glistening spotlight, a woman takes center stage in one of the most touching scenes in all the New Testament. While assuming that her moments of indiscretion in the darkness of night would never be known in the light, suddenly there in the midst of her sin—trapped by her accusers with a death sentence hanging over her head—she encountered Jesus, the Righteous Judge, the Savior of the world. Hers was a lustful, secret sin. But now she realizes that what's done in the dark shall come to the light. Today, she comes face-to-face with Jesus, the Son of God, whose penetrating gaze looked beyond her faults and her disgrace, and saw her desperate need.

It was John, the beloved disciple, who gave us this narrative as part of his record of Christ's ministry in His compassion to broken people. Here he describes a very touching and delicate scene.

Early in the morning as the dawning of a new day unveiled itself, the sound of music was in the air. Songbirds were singing a song written by their Master, the One who taught as no other. Several people were gathering in the temple court to hear Jesus. Jesus came again into the temple, and all the people were coming to Him. He sat down and began to teach them. Suddenly a group of stone-faced scribes and Pharisees interrupted our Lord, dragging a young woman across the pavement and into the great hall. They were the legalist of Israel, all prepped up for another day of fault-finding, judging and condemning others. They had come to make a public example of one that was an outcast who according to their standards didn't belong. What a spectacle it was! She had been caught in the very act of adultery. Notice that they did not bring the man, but only the woman. They caught her in the bed with a man who wasn't her husband.

The woman—who remained anonymous by John in the story—must have stood trembling with fear. Surely she thought her life would end that day. Her head bowed, her shame was great, her body bruised, and her clothing torn. She was their bait to trap Jesus. They hated Him and His teaching. Their plan was to have Him put to death by any means necessary.

Having set her in the center of the court before the crowd of wide-eyed spectators, in claim of the authority of Moses, these false leaders abruptly addressed Jesus saying to Him, *"Teacher, this woman has been caught in adultery, in the very act. Now in the Law Moses commanded us to stone such women; what then do you say?"* (John 8:4-5) Jesus knew that was part of the trap. They were saying this to test Him, so that they might have grounds to accuse Him. Jesus rose to His feet and faced the self-righteous group of hypocrites with their humiliated prisoner in tow. Stooping down, He began writing with His finger on the ground. But when they persisted in asking Him, He straightened up, and said to them, *"He who is without sin among you, let him be the first to throw a stone at her."* (John 8:7) He bowed again and resumed writing. And when they heard this rebuke, they began to go out, one by one, beginning with the older ones, until He was left alone with the woman. Straightening up, Jesus said to her, *"Woman, where are they? Did anyone condemn you?"* And she said, *"No one, Lord."* And Jesus said, *"I do not condemn you either. Go. From now on, sin no more"* (Jn. 8:1-11).

A woman caught in the act of adultery faced public stoning. Moses had written in the Law that if the act occurred in the city, both the man and the woman were to be stoned. Was this woman guilty? Absolutely! They apparently caught her in the very act of having unlawful sexual relation. The Greek word translated "caught" literally means "to seize" or to "overcome," suggesting that her accusers themselves found her in the very act of adultery and apprehended her while still in bed with her partner. But what about the man? Had he escaped? It is not likely, since the religious leaders would have easily outnumbered him. Could he have been a co-conspirator, or worst yet … even one of them who had been put up to the lurid act beforehand! A conspiracy is not out of the question, knowing the hypocrisy of their hearts. They really wanted Jesus; He was the real target. They cared nothing about the woman or her life. At that moment she meant nothing to them, one way or the other. But Jesus knew the hearts of these men. He read their motives like an open book. He sensed their feeble attempt to ensnare Him with His own words.

Had Jesus agreed to the stoning, they could have accused Him of hypocrisy. A man who had been the emblem of compassion and forgiveness would not allow such a harsh penalty. Also, Jesus would have had no legal authority to have her stoned to death since only a Roman official could determine the verdict of death on an individual.

And had He simply demanded she be forgiven and set free, they would have said He was condoning sin and going against the Law of Moses.

"Jesus simply stooped down and with His finger wrote on the ground." (John 8:6) The only time in scripture where we see Jesus writing anything is here in this passage. But what did He write? Did He just scribble in the dust, collecting

His thoughts? But the Greek word translated "word" tells us something more. John recorded that Jesus "wrote" in the sand. The Greek term John uses, which the English renders as "wrote" is "katagrapho."

The last half of that word, grapho, is the verb "to write". The Greek prefix kata can mean "against". In other words it may be that Jesus wrote something in the sand that would have been incriminating to the religious leaders who were present. Could it be that Jesus stooped and began to write out the sins of the woman's accusers in letters large enough for them and others to read? We cannot say for sure that this is what transpired, but if it did, can you imagine the shock of their surprise?

Woman Who Condemns You?
Although there remains a question mark as to what Jesus wrote in the sand, there's no doubt about the meaning of what He said. As the scribes and Pharisees frowned with faces like flint, John tells us that Jesus rose to His feet and said to them, *"He that is without sin among you, let him be the first to throw a stone at her"* (Jn. 8:7) Wow! Talk about shock! I'm sure it struck a cord. As a matter of fact, the text literally reads, "The sinless one of you, first, on her, let him cast a stone." In the Greek, that is nothing short of emphatic. That is, be sure you have no sins against you, and then, you're qualified to bring shame, accusation and even death on this woman. Only make sure your hearts are pure and sinless."

Peter Marshall captures the scene in a vivid manner:

> *Looking into their faces, Christ sees into the yesterdays that lie deep in the pools of memory conscience. He sees into their very hearts, and that moving finger writes on... Idolater... Liar... Drunkard... Murderer... Adulterer... There is the thud of stone after stone falling on the pavement. Not many of the Pharisees are left. One by one,*

The Dark Side of Love

they creep away—like animals—slinking into the shadows…shuffling off into the crowded streets to lose themselves in the multitudes.

Humiliated, they began to slip away, one by one. *"When they heard it, they began to go out one by one, beginning with the older ones, and He was left alone, and the woman, where she was in the center of the court"* (Jn. 8:9). Jesus, after dismissing the accusers, looked directly into the eyes of a woman of the night, just moments before she was standing in the shadow of death, openly exposed and condemned by her accusers. Now she stands before the Light of the World, the Righteous Judge, guilty of adultery. As she met the gaze of the Savior, it is here that the light of heaven's grace eclipses the darkness of sin's shame. It is here that the Balm of Gilead makes the wounded whole. In the history of mankind, has there ever been a more amazing contrast of character? I think that's what makes the final exchange between them so awesome—sinner versus the sinless Son of God; a woman versus the man who was God; and the adulteress versus the Holy One of heaven.

When Jesus had raised Himself up and saw no one but the woman,

Jesus said to her, *"Woman, where are those accusers of yours? "Has anyone condemned you?" She said, "No one, Lord." And Jesus said, "Neither do I condemn you; Go and sin no more"* (Jn. 8:10,11). He was the only one who could condemn her and He would not do so. Instead, He set her free.

Could it be possible that for the first time in her life she stopped condemning herself too? Yes, yes, yes! That's what Jesus does for us; He delivers us from the darkness of sin and cause the sun to shine.

Jesus said, *"What I tell you in the dark, speak in the daylight"* (Matt. 10:27). What does that mean to us? It means, be quiet, listen to God when things are their worst, and you will be able to talk to others when you are better.

Oswald Chambers explained, *"Watch where God puts you in darkness, and when you are there keep your mouth shut... Darkness is the time to listen and heed. If you talk to other people, you cannot hear what God is saying. When you are in the dark, listen, and God will give you a very precious message for someone else when you get in the light."*

Our response to pain is as varied as pain itself. I've heard it said that women can bear more pain than men. In fact, one person wrote: *"Man endures pain as an undeserved punishment; woman accepts it as a natural heritage."* Having watched my wife in pain during the birth of our children, I believe it's true. My mother used to say: *"Death goes around a woman's bed nine times when she's in child-birth."*

In the first little book she wrote, long before she became known throughout the world, Corrie ten Boom told of her experience in Ravensbruk prison during World War 11 ...

> *I did not understand the "why" of suffering, except that of my own suffering in this place. God had brought me here for a specific task. I was here to lead the sorrowing and the despairing to the Savior. I was to see how He comforted them. I was to point the way to heaven to people among whom were many that would be dying....The "why" of my own suffering was no problem to me. This, too, I had learned: that I was not called upon to bear the grief and the cares of the whole world around me. And so I prayed, "Lord teach me to cast all my burdens upon Thee and go on without them. Only Thy Spirit can teach me that lesson. Give me Thy Spirit, O Lord, and I shall have faith, such faith that I shall no longer carry a load of care."*

For Troubled Hearts Only

Where is God when we suffer? He is ever-present, all-knowing, and with us in all our struggles and trials. Nothing that happens in our lives takes God by surprise. We are not alone in the darkness of suffering, for our God loves us; He is a friend that is closer than a brother, and we need not fear the shadows of night for Jesus is our Light.

Although it may seem incredible and even unbelievable, it's true—God wants our companionship; He wants to be close to you. Not like the friends we have who may leave us when the going gets tough. He wants to shield us, to protect us, and to guide us in the path of righteousness through life.

The story was told about a lone survivor of a shipwreck who was marooned on an uninhabited island. He managed to build a hut in which he put everything he had saved from the wreck. He prayed to God for rescue, and anxiously scanned the horizon every day to signal any passing ship. One day he returned to his hut and to his horror found it in flames and all of his possessions gone. What a tragedy! But shortly after, a ship arrived. "We saw your smoke signal and hurried here," the captain explained. The survivor had only seen his burnt hut, but out of disaster, God worked a miracle. The man fell to his knees to thank God for the fire that caused his rescue. Out of the darkness of despair shone a great light. From the smoke God sent a distress call, an S.O.S. call. Was it the dark side of love? I believe it was.

When we go through the fire, He will be with us. God is faithful in His promise to give us beauty for ashes, the oil of joy for mourning, and the garment of praise for the spirit of heaviness (Isa. 61:3). Christ is the Master Comforter. He is the Savior. Are you burned out on life? It may be that all you have left are ashes—the ashes of a broken relationship, the ashes of yesterday's passion. Whatever you're suffering today, please remember that your pain is no mistake. As a matter of fact your suffering may be exactly what Christ will use to bring you to Him, to draw you to His heart and give you peace.

"Jesus!" what a name! It's the name of the Son of God. His name is Jesus. It's the sweetest name I know. Perhaps you have never realized your need for a personal relationship with God, through faith in Jesus Christ.

I suggest you give your heart to Jesus. Come to Him. Admit where you are and express to Him your need of salvation. A simple prayer is all it takes to begin your life-changing relationship with Him. Let's close with a simple prayer that you may speak in your heart to Christ and receive Him into your heart by faith.

Lord Jesus, I know that I'm a sinner. I ask your forgiveness of my sins. Today I come to You, believing that You died for my sins and that You rose from the dead. I turn my back on my sins and on my stubborn ways as I surrender all to You. I accept your forgiveness, and I thank You for Your saving grace, as I accept Your gift of eternal life. Amen.

Chapter 12
The Power of Prayer

☙❧

Sacrifice thank-offerings to God, fulfill your vows to the Most High, and call upon Me in the day of trouble; I will deliver you, and you will honor Me

(Ps. 50:15)

Why worry about it? Pray about it. If you want to worry no more, then by all means, pray more. And after you've said "Amen" ... pray more. Why look forward in fear—pacing the floor and wringing your hands—when you can look upward in faith.

In regards to prayer, the Bible is quite clear, *"...men ought to always pray, and not faint"* (Lu. 18:1). Many people pray only when they are under great stress or in danger. I have been in airplanes during a thunder storm; you could see many praying. There seems to be an instinct in man to pray in times of danger. If we are to pray in times of trouble, we should be people of prayer before the crisis hits.

Prayer should never be an embarrassment. We should never be ashamed of demonstrating our faith, regardless of where we are. Was Christ ashamed to die for us on an old rugged Cross? Think about it! It may be contrary to popular opinion, but sincere prayer is never a show of excessive religiosity. Nor is it a form of emotional entertainment.

Hope For A Troubled Heart

I heard the story of a little mother, who each night would always kneel by her bedside and pray before she turned in for bed. Not one of those quick, "Now I lay me down to sleep" prayers of mere formality, but sincere fervent prayer.

One night as she arrived home, she interrupted a burglary in progress. Unaware of what was transpiring, she got ready for bed. The thief, now hiding under her bed, waited to attack this dear lady. But as she knelt in prayer, in praise unto the Rock of her salvation, in thanksgiving, praying with supplication, praying in the spirit of intercession, she prayed the effectual fervent prayer of a righteous woman of God. Yes, she prayed until the Spirit of God began to move in the room, until the Lord laid His hands on her would-be assailant and arrested and convicted the young man's heart. And as he came out from under the bed, he cried in godly sorrow, "How can I be saved?" That young man received Christ that night because someone prayed for him.

We may have to cry with fear and trembling, but cry in prayer and cry in faith. For *"weeping may endure for a night, but joy comes in the morning"* (Ps. 30:5).

Why are we as Christians, urged to pray? As believers in Christ, prayer is the essence of our lives. God desires a relationship with you—a personal relationship. As a matter of fact, He stands at the door of our hearts and knocks saying: *"Behold, I stand at the door and knock. If any man will hear My voice and opens the door, I will come in to him and dine with him"* (Rev. 3:20). So Christianity is essentially a relationship between God and His people. Relationships are established and maintained by good communication. Prayer is the communication between you and God. We are urged to pray because by doing so we build ourselves up on our most holy faith, which is strengthened by prayer.

Now there are several types of prayer. First, we have the Prayer of Adoration in which we have the awesome privilege of praising God. When the Children of Israel were bringing the Ark of the Covenant into Jerusalem, David danced before the Lord with all his might in an expression of praise to God.

The Power of Prayer

Secondly, it is the "Prayer of Confession", which opens the way to forgiveness and restoration. *"If we confess our sins, He is faithful and just to forgive us our sins and to cleanse us from all unrighteousness"* (Jas. 1:9).

Thirdly, the "Prayer of Thanksgiving": We should give thanks unto the Lord always. Thanking God for what He has done for us will encourage our faith to believe Him today. The fact of the matter is, God delivered us from the power of darkness, from the bondage of sin and translated us into the kingdom of His dear Son, and that is enough to give Him thanks forever!

Then fourthly, there is the "Prayer of Intercession": God is not willing that any should perish, but that all should come to repentance. And when we pray we are to remember others—the hurting, the lost, and the broken. We pray that God would heal the hurt, save the lost, and mend the broken-hearted.

The fifth, point? is the "Prayer of Petition", which grants us permission to pray for ourselves. But it is important to remember the words of Jesus: *"And when you stand praying, if you have anything against anyone, forgive him that your Father in heaven may also forgive you your trespasses. But if you do not forgive, neither will your Father in heaven forgive your trespasses"* (Mark 11:25-26).

But you say: "Wes, how can I do that! When I've been hurt so bad? Well, I'm glad you asked. The Bible says: *"The love of God has been poured out in our hearts by the Holy Spirit who was given to us"* (Rom. 5:5). The ability to forgive is a direct result of the love of God in our hearts, which is produced by the Holy Spirit, which is Christ in you, the Hope of Glory. It is Christ within who grants us the grace to forgive. This is imperative, as faith to remove mountains is nothing without love to forgive.

The greater the pressure, the more Jesus saw the necessity of getting alone in prayer: *"So He Himself often withdrew into the wilderness and prayed."* (Luke 5:16) And if Jesus, being who He was, saw the necessity of prayer, how is it that we think we can survive the pressures of this world without prayer? Jesus showed us that prayer needs to be an essential part of our very being. We need to depend upon the strength that comes from a life of prayer. Luke gives us so much insight into the prayer-life of Jesus. He mentioned that as Jesus was baptized, He was praying when the Spirit descended upon Him. He also tells us in Luke 6:12, that Jesus prayed all night before selecting the twelve apostles. It is so important to be directed by God in choosing leadership and to spend time with Him in prayer.

My mother has always been a real prayer-warrior. One evening while Delores was over to mom's house, she felt a sudden pain in her chest. The pain was so severe that it literally buckled her knees. Mom, upon hearing her faint cry, rushed to her aid in prayer, and with just a touch of her hand, God answered, her healing was immediate and the pain was gone. O thanks be unto God! He answers prayer!

In 1 Thessalonians 5:16,17, Paul provides two exhortations.

First, "rejoice always." What does that mean? It means the Church should be a people of joy. We ought to be the most joyful people on this planet because God has forgiven our sins, and we have the hope of eternal life through Jesus Christ.

Secondly, the Church should be a praying Church ... *"Pray without ceasing."* (1 Thess. 5:17) Paul isn't saying we have to be on our knees all day. Prayer is a sincere desire of my heart; in constant communion and fellowship with God. It's the awe of His Wonder and Majesty that I experience in worship of Him.

Prayer is the power that delivers. Many of us today are weak in prayer. And the pride of learning and "self" achievements is so often against the dependent humility of prayer. Prayer is not a performance for the routine of service. As Christians we must make prayer our daily bread, for without it we are weak and powerless in our witness for Christ.

In the tenth chapter of Acts, Dr. Luke tells us about a man named Cornelius. Cornelius was a Roman soldier and a devout man as well. That simply means he was righteous. It's good to be a soldier, but it's better to be a righteous soldier.

There are two striking characteristics about Cornelius that we notice. First, he feared God. He had a reverential respect for God that caused him to walk uprightly before the true Living God. The Bible says, "By mercy and truth iniquity is purged and by the fear of the Lord men depart from evil" (Prov.16:6). Secondly, he was a man of prayer. It's interesting that although he had not heard the gospel, he was a man of prayer. So he was a righteous man, meaning that he did what was right in the eyes of God, and he prayed all the time.

Cornelius must have heard someone share the word, because faith comes by hearing and hearing by the Word of God. Notice how his prayer-life and his generosity to the poor brought him into the favor of God. The fruit of prayer is righteousness. Furthermore, Peter declares in verse thirty-four and thirty five, *"In truth I perceive that God is not a respecter of persons, but in every nation whoever fears Him and works righteousness is accepted by Him."*

When Jesus told the story about the widow and the unjust judge, it was to the intent that men ought to always pray and not faint. In the story, He illustrates the reward of persistence. The little woman had a problem with her adversary. It was of such proportion that she needed help from this particular judge. He was not a righteous man, but one who was unjust. He did not fear God, nor did he regard man. Nevertheless, this little woman came asking for his help. At first, he refused and turned her away. But her persistent petition wearied the judge to the point where he exclaimed, "Give her what she wants!" Now contrast the unjust judge with our loving heavenly Father. The parable is to encourage faith in God as we persist in prayer.

What about Prayer for the Sick?
There is a law of scriptural interpretation that says: If it was taught by Jesus, practiced in the book of Acts, and there is

a teaching on it in the epistles, then we accept it for general church practice through the Church's history.

The Bible plainly states that Jesus went about doing good; and healing all who were oppressed of the devil. So we see the healing of the sick in the ministry of our Lord; and it was very common. Prayer for the sick was practiced in the early Church by the apostles as well. The Apostle James admonishes us to pray for the sick saying, *"Is any sick among you? Let him call for the elders of the church; and let them pray over him, anointing him with oil in the name of the Lord: And the prayer of faith shall save the sick, and the Lord shall raise him up..."* (Jas. 5:14,15).

Years ago, a woman brought her son, who was born without a hip socket to an Oral Robert's crusade, asking Dr. Robert's to pray that God would heal the young boy. But after hearing her request, he confessed, "I don't have the faith for a creative miracle; you'll have to wait for the resurrection." But the little mother would not be denied saying, "Brother Roberts, I'm not asking you to have the faith. I'll do the believing; I m just asking you to pray. So he prayed seemingly to no avail, as there was no physical change in the young lad's condition. But the next night as Dr. Roberts arrived and entered the crusade, he saw this young fellow leaping and jumping on the platform. "What's going on?" "Well, that's the young boy you prayed for last night," replied his attendant. And as he examined what should have been a hollow area in the boy's side, it was now filled in with a new hip socket. "What happened?" His mother responded, "I took him to the doctor that delivered him at birth and he said, 'He's got a new hip socket!'" The crowd went wild as they all rejoiced over what God had done.

The Power of Prayer

Unction must come done from heaven and spread a savor and feeling and relish over... ministry;... The Bible must hold the first place, and the last also must be given to the Word of God and prayer.

Richard Cecil

The Attitude of Prayer

Jesus told a parable in Luke 18:9-14, to address two different attitudes of prayer—"some who trusted in themselves that they were righteousness, and despised others" there was a Pharisee and a tax-collector who both went to the temple to pray. The Pharisee was bragging to God about what a wonderful person he was, and how he was so much better than others. His prayer was self-centered, all about him, and he kept praying a selfish, boastful prayer. The tax-collector, on the other hand, knew he was a sinner and humbly cried out for mercy. Which one was justified? Yes, the tax-collector was justified, which means he was declared righteous.

The lesson we learn is simply this ... We can either come to God in our own righteousness (which is by the way as filthy rages) or we can come in repentance and brokenness and receive the righteousness of Christ.

The All Sufficient One

The apostle Paul had his share of critics' to his ministry; men who would follow him around seeking to reap the benefits of his labor. Men who were prime examples of those who trusted in themselves that they were righteous, who sought to live off the church as opposed to developing the body of Christ. The body of Christ is not expanded in transferring members from one church to another. If we are to expand the body of Christ, we must go out and break fresh ground and bring others to Jesus Christ, that they too might know Him. These men were seeking to discredit Paul in the eyes of the people. Such was the case in Corinth; Those who followed Paul; and were seeking to uproot his ministry; disputing his message on the gospel of grace; looking to bring the people under the Law. They were challenging his authority as an apostle. So Paul was always defending himself against his critics'.

So here again in chapter three we find the apostle responding to these men saying; *"Do we begin again to commend ourselves? Or need we, as some others, epistles of commendation to you, or letters of commendation from you? You are our epistle written in our hearts, known and read of all men:"* Your faith in Jesus Christ is all the commendation I need. You are proof of my apostleship. The fact of your existence as a church is all the recommendation I need to prove the authenticity of my calling. *"Forasmuch as you are manifestly declared to be the epistle of Christ ministered by us, written not with ink, but with the Spirit of the living God; not in tables of stone, but in fleshy tables of the heart. And such trust we have through Christ to God-ward:"* (2 Corinthians 3:1-4).

> *Not that we are sufficient of ourselves to think of anything as being from ourselves, but our sufficiency is from God, who also made us sufficient as ministers of the new covenant, not of the letter but of the Spirit; for the letter kills but the Spirit gives life*

(2 Corinthians 3:5)

I can't count the times when facing the issues of the ministry; I've cried out to God; "Oh Lord, without you I can do nothing." Am I Inadequate? Yes I 'am. Sometimes God allows us to come to the end of our own capacities, so that we might learn to depend on and trust in Him. God revealed Himself to Abraham as El Shaddai; which means the all sufficient One. I 'am inept and unable to do the work of the Lord in my own strength. But He is able and all sufficient to do exceedingly abundantly above all that I ask or think,

The Power of Prayer

according to the power that works in me. Paul said He is the One who has made us able ministers of this new testament; not of the letter, but of the spirit: for the letter killeth, but the spirit giveth life.

Now don't misunderstand what Paul is saying here, and take this scripture out of context. The letter in teaching the Word of God does not kill. The bible tells us that the Word of God is alive and powerful, sharper than a two-edged sword, piercing to the dividing asunder of soul and spirit, and of the joints and marrow, and is a discerner of the thoughts and intents of the heart (Heb. 4:12). The amplified version says: "*For the Word that God speaks is alive and full of power [making it active, operative, energizing, and effective]; it is sharper than any two-edged sword, penetrating to the dividing line of the breath of life (soul) and [the immortal] spirit, and of joints and marrow [of the deepest parts of our nature], exposing and sifting and analyzing and judging the very thoughts and purposes of the heart.*"

The letter that kills is the letter of the law. And Paul here declares that he is the able minister of the New Testament; the new covenant. The old covenant was by the law. And the old covenant in the letter of the law condemns us to death. If you want to be righteous before God by the keeping of the law it is too late, for it has already condemned you to death. The letter of the law kills. For the law says he that does these things shall live by them. But it also says if you keep the whole law and violate it in one point, you're guilty of all, and so the law condemns every one of us to death. But it is the spirit in the new covenant that brings us life.

We must, therefore, remember that we are not sufficient in ourselves to do the work of God! He is the only One who is sufficient and we need Him if we are to do anything for the up-building of the kingdom of God. The letter of the Law which kills is militant, straight forward, and hard as stone, and often referred to as legalism. Jesus referred to it, speaking to His disciples He said: *"Beware of the leaven of the Pharisees..."* (Matthew 16:11-12). It is nothing more than dead conservatism—too dead to speculate; too dead to think, study, or to pray. It maybe scholarly and critical as were the Scribes and Pharisees, or may come across as charismatic in its expression, but it can't give us life.

Some people study the Law as a lawyer studies textbooks, to form a brief or to defend a case. It is likened to a cold winter's frost, a killing frost. You can dress it up with poetry and fancy rhetoric, and sprinkle it with a little dab of prayer, spiced with a dash of sensationalism, and illuminated by genius. But these are at best the rare and beautiful flowers which coffin the dead corpse. The letter of the Law deals with only the surface of things; but it never goes deep to penetrate the inner-parts. The Spirit is the one distinguishing feature that separates true gospel preaching from all other methods of presenting the truth. The Spirit confirms and reveals truth with all the power of God.

When we seek to become righteous by obeying the law, it can only allow you to follow the letter of the law, as best you can. But even if we are good at obeying the rules, there will still be something missing.

God wants to have a relationship with you, and relationships aren't based on rules, but on love, *"because the love of God has been poured out in our hearts by the Holy Ghost who was given to us"* (Rom. 5:5). This is the very reason Jesus was so attractive to people, while the religious leaders, the Pharisees were so unattractive. The Pharisees were following the letter of the Law, while completely missing the Spirit. The Lord Jesus embodied the Spirit of the Law. His was a love so natural, as opposed to the hypocritical religion of the Pharisees.

If we live by the letter of the Law we will always end up frustrated and condemned to death. But living in the Spirit will always lead to an abundant life that is lived in a loving relationship with God.

Chapter 13
Blessed Hope

☙❧

The Jewish leaders had developed a complicated interpretation of the Old Testament Law that was utterly ridiculous. If you had false teeth in your mouth or nails in your sandals, you couldn't wear them on the Sabbath. It would be considered carrying a burden, because of their weight.

In the ninth chapter of John's gospel, we read: *"Now as Jesus passed by, He saw a man who was blind from birth. And His disciples asked Him, saying, 'Rabbi, who sinned, this man or his parents, that he was born blind?' Jesus answered, 'Neither this man nor his parents sinned, but that the works of God should be revealed in him. I must work the works of Him who sent Me while it is day; the night is coming when no one can work. As long as I am in the world, I am the light of the world. When He had said these things, He spat on the ground and made clay with the salvia; and He anointed the eyes of the blind man with the clay. And He said to him, 'Go wash in the pool of Siloam' (which is translated, "Sent"). So he went and washed, and came back seeing"* (John 9:1-7).

When Jesus encountered this blind man, His disciples asked Him whose sin had caused the blindness. Jesus answered; *"Neither this man nor his parents sinned, but that the works of God should be revealed in him."* (John 9:3)

At times God allows us to go through difficulty, hardship, and suffering in order that He might accomplish His works in our lives. The Apostle Paul said in regards to his sufferings, *"I consider that the sufferings of this present time are not worthy to be compared with the glory which shall be revealed in us."* (Rom. 8:18)

On this occasion, Jesus intentionally violated the Sabbath regulations in at least two ways. He healed the blind man, which the Jewish leaders viewed as improper on the Sabbath; they considered this work, which was prohibited on the Sabbath. Then, He spit and made clay, and they taught that to make clay on the Sabbath was a violation of the Sabbath Laws. He went out of His way to break their rules to show that He was Lord of the Sabbath. He was the One who had given the Law.

The Jews were trying to pin the healed man down in his explanation as to what happened to him and exactly how he received his sight on the Sabbath day. *"What did He do to you? How did He open your eyes?"* (Rom. 8:26) But he didn't get caught up in their theological debate; instead He offered an argument that was impossible to refute … *"Though I was blind, now I see."* (Rom. 8:25)

It is tough to argue with that kind of evidence. The kind of apologetics that is most effective is the personal attestation that, *"I was blind but now I see; I was dead, but now I'm alive."* (Rom. 8:25)

One vital key to the Christian faith is the hope God gives us. He is always holding out that hope for the future.

In Jeremiah 16:15, the prophet had just spoken of the horrendous darkness that his people, the children of Israel, were facing. The enemy was going to come and destroy the city and the remnant of the people who were not slain would be taken away captive to Babylon. This would be a very dark and bleak picture of the future. But then his vision extended out beyond that. God would still expand His grace and mercy to their children, or their grandchildren, and they would come back from their captivity. They would return, restored by God into their land.

Blessed Hope

Once again, the world is facing a very desolate future. There is going to be a time of great tribulation upon this earth such as the earth has never seen before, or will ever see again. The tribulation will last seven years, and is undoubtedly the worst onslaught of tragedy that the earth will ever experience.

I can almost hear you asking, *"Why? Why would God allow this to happen again?"* (Matthew 24:9-21) Well, I'm glad you asked. God has a three-fold purpose for this period: First, to save and allow many of the Jews who will enter the Millennium to experience the fulfillment of the kingdom promises to Israel made by God, which He swore to Abraham in His covenant (Genesis 17:1-8).

Secondly, to save a multitude of Gentiles who will be allowed entrance into the Millennium kingdom (Matthew 25:31-46, Isaiah 11:6-9).

Thirdly, to pour out judgment on unbelieving mankind and those nations who reject Christ. Jesus said in Matthew. *"And whosoever shall fall on this stone shall be broken: but on whomsoever it shall fall, it will grind him to powder."* (Matthew 21:44) When we throw ourselves on the mercy of Christ, it is with a broken heart and a contrite spirit. And godly sorrow works repentance unto salvation. Then, we will know Him as the *"smitten Rock of Calvary"* – Who was *"wounded for our transgressions, He was bruised for our iniquities: the chastisement for our peace was upon Him; and by His stripes we are healed"* (Isa. 53:5,6). But all who reject His mercy will ultimately face Him in the judgment as the smiting Rock (Revelation 19:11-16).

What is the master passion of your life? Is your life directed by God's plan? The potential to be and to do is God-given. This wonderful gift must not lie dormant within you—unused and unappreciated? You say, "But Wes, you don't understand—I'm under so much stress!" Yes, but is it unnecessary stress? Maybe the yoke you've taken upon yourself is too difficult and the burden you bare—too heavy. Jesus said: "Take My yoke upon you and learn of Me, for My yoke is easy and My burden is light."

Hope For A Troubled Heart

I want you to hear the promises of these verses in Isaiah 41:9,10, as if God is speaking to you personally right now. No matter what difficulty or hardships you may be facing this week, God has chosen you as His servant. And you are His child. *"You whom I have taken from the ends of the earth, and called from its farthest regions, and said to you, 'You are My servant, I have chosen you and have not cast you away: Fear not, for I am with you; Be not dismayed, for I am your God. I will strengthen you, Yes, I will help you, I will uphold you with My righteous right hand.'"* God has called you His. And as you are looking at the barriers that seem to block your progress right now, and as you scan the prospects for the next week, I want you to hear the Lord saying, *"Fear not, for I am with you; Be not dismayed, for I am your God, I will strengthen you, Yes, I will help you, I will uphold you with My righteous hand."* (Isaiah 41:10)

The story was told of two roofers who were working on the same roof, at the same time, doing the same job, and receiving the same pay. The roof was slanted. The one roofer has a safety belt fastened around his waist, with a rope anchored to a secure spot on the other side, while the other guy has only his hands and feet to keep him from falling off. My question is: At the end of the day, which of the two goes home with less stress? Yes, you got it—the one with the safety belt. You see the one roofer was secure in the knowledge he was being held on to, whereas his buddy had no such peace at all.

Who's holding you? Are you just barely holding on—trying to make a hundred for "ninety-nine and a half won't do"?

Jesus said, *"My sheep listen to my voice; I know them, and they follow Me."* (John 10:27-28) I give them eternal life, and they shall never perish; no one can snatch them out of My hand. *"My Father, Who has given them to Me, is greater than all; no one can snatch them out of My Father's hand."* (v. 29) In his letter to the Philippians, Paul assures us that we can be ... *"confident of this very thing, that He who has begun a good work in you will complete it until the day of Jesus Christ."* (Phil. 1:6) God has started a good work in you, and He will not give up. He is not going to stop!

The Lord will perform His perfect work in our lives. He will keep working in you until you see Jesus Christ, either when you go to heaven to be with Him or when He catches up the saints in the rapture. The work of the Spirit of God will continue in you. It is a promise of God, based on His faithfulness. And He hasn't brought you this far to leave you now!

Yes, I know the recession is upon us and the struggle to support our families has been difficult to say the least. Insurance rates have gone through the roof; taxes, inflation, and many other draining on our finances have had negative effects on our lives. And so we live under the illusion, that if I had more money I would be happy. But life is not about more money; some things money can't buy.

> *One hour of eternity, one moment with the Lord,*
> *will make us utterly forget a lifetime of desolations.*
>
> *Horatius Bonar*

It was 1931. The Rev. and Mrs. R. Porteous were taken as prisoners by Chinese communist bandits, and led to a lonely spot on top of a hill where they were to be executed. As they stopped, the leader said, "This is the place." The executioner took a long knife from its holder and raised it above the necks of the courageous couple. Certainly death seemed imminent. However, instead of cringing and begging for mercy, the couple began to sing. The bandits stared with open-mouthed astonishment as they heard this hymn:

Face to Face

Face to face with Christ, my Savior,
Face to face—what will it be,
When with rapture I behold Him,
Jesus Christ who died for me.

Carrie E. Breck

They were ready for death, and thought that would be their last song. But much to their surprise, no order was given. The executioner returned the knife to its place, and the couple was released. Afterwards, they told the story of the perfect peace the Lord Jesus gave them in the face of certain death.

I Can Do All Things through Christ Who Strengthens Me

The Hubble Space Telescope sends back infrared images of faint galaxies that are perhaps twelve-billion light-years away (twelve billion times six trillion miles). Astronomers venture a feeble estimate that the number of stars in the universe equals the number of grains of all the beaches of the world.

The star Betelgeuse has a diameter of 100 million miles, which is larger than the earth's orbit around the sun. It is the brightest star in Orion and marks the western shoulder of the constellation. Betelgeuse emits nearly 7,500 times as much energy as the sun. The combination of size and temperature tells astronomers that the star is a kind of star called a "red super giant."

You say, "Wes, why the enormity? Why such astronomical immensity? Why such vast, unexplored, and unmeasured space?" So that you and I, although astonished, could be stirred by this resolve: "I can do all things through Christ which strengthens me." The Christ of the galaxies is the Christ of your hope for eternal life.

As we contemplate the future—what makes it glorious? It is the gospel. Apostle Paul in 1 Corinthians15:1-8 summed up what the gospel is. The word "gospel" means "good news". What is the good news that Paul was preaching?

First of all, Christ died for our sins according to the scriptures. This is called the "substitutionary atonement". He took our sins on Himself and died in our place. He took our guilt and the punishment we deserved.

Secondly, He was buried. This too was prophesied in that same chapter in verse 9, which says, "They made His grave with the wicked—but with the rich at His death."

Thirdly, He rose from the dead on the third day and was seen by many witnesses including Paul himself.

There are those today who do not believe that Jesus rose from the dead. This is nothing new as there were those in Apostle Paul's day who said the same thing. Apostle Paul made it clear in 1 Corinthians 15:12-20, that if Jesus had not risen from the dead, then we are yet in our sins, hopelessly lost.

A church without a risen Lord is dismal and sad, and any preaching that denies the Resurrection is vain. The Apostle went on to say, "But now Christ is risen from the dead! Hallelujah!"

Daniel was told in chapter 12:13; *"You shall rest, and will arise to your inheritance at the end of the days."*

Jesus told the story about a beggar named Lazarus and the rich man. From this story, which I personally believe is a true story, we learn much about life after death and especially about what happened to people who died before Jesus rose from the dead. I often wonder who laid Lazarus at the gate of a stranger, being full of sores and no longer able to care for himself. Was it his church? When his strength failed and [if you'll allow me to use my sanctified imagination or to paraphrase] his wife left him for another younger man, did they lay him at the rich man's gate? Was it his "fair- weather friends?—those for whom he prayed when they were sick? Was he forced into an early retirement and laid at the gate of Human Social Services, subjected to a debilitating system only to be denied medical insurance?

A saint may get weary on his rocky pilgrim journey, but you can be sure of this one thing, He will rise again.

We learned that there were two destinies—a place of torment and flames and a place of comfort and paradise called "Abraham's Bosom". Abraham was in paradise—"the place of comfort". There was a great gulf between the two locations so that once you went to either destination you couldn't go to the other. Your fate was sealed. Those on the other hand who were in torment and flames had memories of their life on the earth and were quite aware of the choices that were made that contributed to their awful destiny. During this time, the righteous were not able to come into the presence of God, but were in a holding place, the paradise section of the grave located in the heart of the earth. There they were receiving comfort, waiting for deliverance.

My friend, death is not the end of the story. Apostle Paul wrote in Ephesians 4:8-10 concerning the Lord Jesus: *"When He ascended on high, He led captivity captive, and gave gifts to men."* He continued on to say that Jesus ascended after He "first descended into the lower parts of the earth" and that He then "ascended far above all the heavens, that He might fulfill all things." So, after Jesus died, He led the captives from their captivity and took them with Him, transferring paradise from the heart of the earth to heaven itself. Before the death of Jesus, the saints who died were unable to go into the presence of God. They had to wait for the atonement of their sins at the Cross of Christ.

When Jesus died, the door to heaven was opened, and He personally escorted them all the way there. A child of God who dies today doesn't need to go to Abraham's Bosom. Since the price of our sin has now been paid, we go immediately into the presence of the Lord in heaven. For us, being absent from the body is to be present with the Lord (2 Corinthians 5:8).

The term "sleep" is used in the New Testament to refer to the death of a Christian. There's no doubt it began with Jesus. When Mary and Martha, sent word to Jesus that their brother Lazarus was sick (John 11:3,6), talking to His disciples, Jesus said, *"Our friend Lazarus sleeps"* (Jn. 11:11). His disciples said, *"If he sleeps, he will get well"* (v. 12). But then Jesus told them plainly that Lazarus was dead (v. 14).

Jesus used the term "sleep" because what happens to a child of God is not the same thing that happens to a sinner who dies. Jesus told Martha, *"I am the resurrection and the life. He who believes in Me, though he may die, he shall live. And whoever lives and believes in Me shall never die"* (Jn. 11:25). Jesus was referring to spiritual death, which is the separation of consciousness from God. He was saying that anyone who believes in Him will never be consciously separated from God!

Jesus Is Coming
The words "caught up" are a translation of the Greek word harpazo. Harpazo means "to be snatched away or taken away by force". We will be taken away by the force of God's Spirit at the call of Jesus. We'll be caught up, together with our loved ones, who died in Christ, to meet the Lord in the air.

Now don't mistake this for the second coming of Jesus, it's not His second coming. He is coming for His Church prior to His second coming with His Church. There will be a seven-year period of time when we will be with the Lord in heaven. Then when He returns to earth, we'll come back and reign with Him for a thousand years, and we will ever be with the Lord.

Paul said we are to comfort one another with these words. And not to sorrow as those who have no hope. We are to set our affections and our minds on the eternal glories that God has for those of us who walk in fellowship with Him. I thank God that we have an inheritance laid up for us. Is your reservation in? Is your place reserved?

Peter said, *"Blessed be the God and Father of our Lord Jesus Christ, who according to His abundant mercy has begotten us again to a living hope through the resurrection of Jesus Christ from the dead, to an inheritance incorruptible and undefiled and that does not fade away, reserved in heaven for you, who are kept by the power of God through faith for salvation ready to be revealed in the last time"* (1 Pet. 1:3-5).

Are you in that place of having received forgiveness right now? Have you trusted Jesus Christ as your Savior? My friend, you can start over right now and receive His forgiveness and eternal life, which is our blessed hope. Just ask. He's waiting.

Chapter 14
The Invitation

☙❧

You are invited to a secret place. Where? "The secret place of the Most High." Can I live there? I need a place to stay. Yes, you can dwell there. Where was that? "Under the shadow of the Almighty." Sometimes, I'm afraid; the thought of terrorism frightens me. Can you say of the Lord ... He is my Refuge, and my fortress; My God in Him I will trust. *"He shall cover you with His Feathers, And under His wings you shall take refuge: His truth shall be your shield and buckler. You shall not be afraid of the terror by night, nor of the arrow that flies by day, nor of the pestilence that walks in darkness, nor of the destruction that lays waste at noonday"* (Ps. 91:1-6).

RSVP—Please respond. The thought of terrorism frightens me, and I'm afraid of the dark.

What about protection? RSVP—Please Respond.

When you receive an invitation, it is considered an honor—to be held in high regard. I believe that all invitations deserve at least a thoughtful response.

But the most incredible invitations are not found in Madison Avenue Advertisements, nor in envelopes and not even from Oprah. They are found in the Bible. God has been offering invitations since the beginning of time. He invited Adam to the Garden of Eden, Noah and his family to enter the ark, Moses to the mountain top, and David to shepherd His sheep. He invited Israel to leave the bondage of Egypt and come into the Promise Land. God is a God of invitation.

Through the angel Gabriel, God invited a young virgin girl to give birth to His son, the Messiah. He invited Peter to drop his net and fish for men. He invited a woman at Jacob's Well to drink from a fountain that never runs dry. He invited Mary Magdalene to start over again, and Thomas to touch His wounds.

Not only does God invite us, but He is also the King who prepares the table. David said, *"You prepare a table before me..."* (Psalm 23:5). He sets the table and invites His subjects to come in. Well, what's on the menu: bread—the staff of life. But this is not just any bread. Jesus contrasted Himself with the manna that came down from heaven during the time of Moses. The manna provided temporary sustenance for the people, just as Jesus had done the day before by feeding five thousand with two small fish and five barley loaves of bread. They were invited to sit and dine at the King's table. But physical sustenance is not what people ultimately need.

When God revealed Himself to Moses, He identified Himself as the *"I AM." Now Jesus said, "I AM the bread of life."* (John 6:48)

God is the King who prepares the palace. How great is the King Who invites even the poorest of the poor to His palace?

It is the regularity, not so much the uniqueness, of God's great wonders that causes them to be so staggering. Rather than shocking the globe with an occasional display of His deity, God has opted to demonstrate His power on a daily basis: rolling thunder; crashing waves; an array of dazzling colors; the miracle of birth; the exhilaration of life. We are surrounded by miracles. God is inviting us to behold His glory, throwing testimonies at us like fireworks, each one exploding, proclaiming ... God is great, Great is our God!

The psalmist marveled at such holy handiwork. *"The heavens declare the glory of God and the firmament shows and proclaims His handiwork"* (Ps. 19:1). But still He calls. He invites those cast down, weak and worn: *"Lift up your heads, O ye gates, and be lifted up you everlasting doors and the King of glory shall come in"* (Ps. 24:7).

The Invitation

Dorothy invited her new found friends to follow the Yellow-Brick Road. You remember the story in The Wonderful Wizard of Oz. But what did they discover at the end of their journey? Not a "wonderful wizard", for the wizard was a wimp—nothing more than smoke and mirrors and tin-drum thunder. That is not what you need, nor what you're looking for. To carry the burden of a god who can't even carry himself is absurd. My friend, you don't need that—a god in a box, or a god in a bottle, or a god in a fantasized Hollywood script. You're invited to enter the strait gate, walk up the King's highway by a God who placed one hundred billion stars in the galaxies and called each one by their name. The same God who shaped two balls of flesh into seventy-five to one hundred billion nerve cells, each with as many as ten-thousand connections to other nerve cells, then placed it in a skull, and called it a brain. He is the Lord of host, vast and transcendent. Yet, as great as He is, He invites us to come. All who are weary, all who are weak, all who are heavy-laden, come.

The prophet Isaiah declared: *"The wilderness and the waste shall be glad for them, and the desert shall rejoice and blossom as the rose; It shall blossom abundantly and rejoice, even with joy and singing. The glory of Lebanon shall be given to it, the excellence of Carmel and Sharon. They shall see the glory of the Lord, the splendor of our God"* (Isa. 35:1,2).

What a blessed future awaits believers of all the ages in the new heaven, and the new earth as well. That being said, I could not close without a final invitation to you as a reader, to be absolutely sure that you belong to Christ.

In the last six verses of the book of Revelation, we find one of the most compelling invitations to repent of sin and receive Jesus Christ as Lord and Savior than anywhere in the Bible. "*I, Jesus, initiate this final biblical invitation.*" (Rev. 22:16).

"*I, Jesus, have sent My angel to testify to you these things in the churches.*" (Rev. 22:16). "*I am the Root and the Offspring of David, the Bright and Morning Star.*" The Lord Jesus

Himself wants John to make it very clear—after picturing a panorama of scenes covering the past, present, and future, and after peering deep into the heavens, the earth and hell, after being introduced to the Son of God, to man all the way from his best to his worst state and to the devil himself— Jesus wants and has the last word! Why? Because, as we read in chapter one, verse five, He is the one above all others "who loves us and has freed us from our sins by His blood" shed on the Cross for our sins, to purchase our pardon and peace. And therefore, He is the One to whom we are ultimately accountable to— He also states in Revelations, *"I am the First and the Last. I am He who lives, and was dead, and behold, I am alive forevermore. Amen. And I have the keys of Hades and of death."* (Rev. 1:17-18)

Jesus continues His invitation, in chapter three, verse twenty, as He declares: *"Behold, I stand at the door and knock; If anyone hears My voice and opens the door, I will come in to him and dine with him and he with Me."* Jesus is saying to you right now open your heart and I will come in. My friend, as you read this book, it is the Holy Spirit who has inspired you to give your life to Jesus. Can you here Him? *"Come!"* Come to Christ! In verse seventeen we read that *"The Spirit and the bride say, Come!"* The bride of Christ is His Church. It consists of those who have received Him as Lord and Savior. As a loving shepherd, He has promised to provide for all of our needs. We are the bride! He is the bridegroom!

Again, Jesus invites, *"Let him who hears say, 'Come!'"* (Rev. 22:17).

The Apostle Paul tells us in Romans 10:17, that *"faith comes by hearing the message, and the message is heard through the Word of God."* Jesus says in John's gospel, *"I tell you the truth, whoever hears My word and believes Him who sent Me, has eternal life and shall not be condemned; he has passed from death unto life."* (John 5:24)

"And let him who thirst come. Whoever desires, let him take the water of life freely" (Rev. 22:17). Pascal, the great French physicist and philosopher of the seventeenth century, said

The Invitation

that all humans have in their hearts a God-shaped void that only Jesus Christ can fill.

Once again, Jesus repeats the invitation for a final time with, I believe, the strongest and ever so earnest call, *"And whoever desires, let him take the water of life freely."* Your decision for Christ is a matter of your will. God has done everything possible to bring you salvation; you can't add anything to what He has done. If you want to be saved and go to heaven, you can, by believing and accepting the Lord Jesus Christ as your Savior. When you are really serious concerning your commitment to Christ, not just in passing, but as an ongoing relationship, you will have Him as your Lord and Savior forever (1 Thessalonians 4:17).

If you have never invited Him, as Lord and Savior into your life, you need to do so now, and the good news is you can do so now!

You say, "But Wes, I'm having such a difficult time in my life right now, you don't know what I'm going through." Well, I believe that God often uses difficulties and heartaches that come into our lives to show us our need for Christ. Maybe it's a business disappointment, or a broken marriage, a shattered dream, a tragic heartache, a severed relationship between you and your children. Listen, whatever the disappointment, it's His appointment!

Jesus is knocking at your heart's door, but you, and you alone have to respond. Right now, you can bow your head, wherever you are: on an airplane, in your home, in an office, in a jail, in a hospital. Maybe you're in a hotel, but you can open your heart to Jesus Christ by a simple prayer of faith.

So we have this good news made possible by Christ's everlasting love, by His death on the Cross for us. And we have His knocking on our heart's door in the present, seeking entrance into our lives.

Remember, the "Righteousness based on faith [imputed by God and bringing right relationship with Him] says …

Do not say in your heart, who will ascend into heaven? That is, to bring Christ down from above; Or who will descend into the abyss? That is, to bring Christ up from the dead). But what does it say? "The Word is near you, in your mouth and in your heart" (that is the word of faith which we preach): that if you confess with your mouth the Lord Jesus and believe in your heart that God has raised Him from the dead, you will be save. For with the heart one believes unto righteousness and with the mouth confession is made unto salvation. The Word (the message, the basis and object) of faith which we preach, Because if you acknowledge and confess with your mouth that Jesus is Lord and in your heart believe (adhere to, trust in, and rely on the truth) that God raised Him from the dead, you will be saved. For with the heart a person believes (adheres to, trust in, and relies on Christ) and so is justified (declared righteous, acceptable to God), and with the mouth he confesses (declares openly and speaks out freely his faith) and confirms his salvation."

(Rom. 10:6-10)

The reason that Jesus came to earth was that we might have life through his death as the definitive sacrifice for sin. God desires to have a relationship with you. He desires to reveal Himself to you, to shower His loving-kindness upon you. God wants you to live with Him forever.

The choice is yours. You have a will of your own and God will respect your right to tell Him "No". And you can reject Jesus Christ and choose instead the path of sin. But He also loves you enough to warn you of the perils of turning away. In Revelation chapter 21, He makes it very clear that *"the cowardly, the unbelieving, the abominable, the murderers, sexually immoral, sorcers, idolaters, and all liars—shall have*

The Invitation

their part in the lake which burns with fire and brimstone," Then He adds, *"This is the second death"* (Rev. 21:8).

But the Bible concludes with a promise in Revelation 22:21, for all who accept Christ: *"The grace of our Lord Jesus Christ be with you all. Amen."* What more could you ever hope for than that the grace of our Lord Jesus Christ be with you forever? He will be with you, always, graciously giving you His unmerited favors.

Now let's pray ...

Dear Lord Jesus, forgive me for all my sins. I believe that you died on the Cross, was buried, and on the third day, God the Father raised You from the dead. Right now Lord Jesus, I open the door to my heart, and I receive you into my heart, as my Lord and Savior, Amen.

> *But as many as received Him, to them He gave the right to become the children of God, to those who believe in His name: who were born, not of blood, nor of the will of the flesh, nor of the will of man, but of God.*
>
> *(Jn. 1:12,13)*
>
> *You asked me how I gave my heart to Christ, I do not know. There came a yearning for Him in my soul so long ago. I found earth's flowers would fade and die, I wept for something that would satisfy and then, and then, somehow I seemed to dare to lift my broken heart to God in prayer. I do not know, I cannot tell you how; I only know, He is my Savior now.*
>
> *Anonymous*

Bibliography

Aggrey, James. *Parable of the Eagle*. Print.

Allen, James X. *Put Away Aimlessness and Weakness, and to Begin to Think with Purpose*. Lovequotes.com, 28 Jan. 2011. Web. 06 Jan. 2014.

Ansari, Azadeh X. "Climate Change." *'Climate Change' Forces Eskimos to Abandon Village*. Cable News Network, 28 Apr. 2009. Web.

"Battle Hymn of the Republic." *Battle Hymn of the Republic*. Web. 26 Jan. 2014.

Breck, Carrie E. "Face to Face with Christ, My Savior." *Face to Face with Christ, My Savior*. CD.

Brunner, Emil. "Emil Brunner." *: What Oxygen Is to the Lungs, Such Is Hope to the Meaning of Life*. Brain Media Limited. Web. 06 Jan. 2014.

Carlyle, Thomas. "Quotation Details." *The Quotations Page*. Quotations Page. Web. 06 Jan. 2014.

Carmichael, Amy. "Witnesses to Hope." *Witnesses to Hope*. The Confit Theme. Web. 07 Jan. 2014.

"Charles Kettering Quotes." *BrainyQuote*. Xplore. Web. 07 Jan. 2014.

Chisolm, Thomas O. "Great Is Thy Faithfulness." *Great Is Thy Faithfulness*. Hope Publishing Company, 1923. Vinyl recording.

Coolidge, Calvin. "Calvin Coolidge Quotes." *BrainyQuote*. Xplore. Web. 07 Jan. 2014.

Danby, Herbert. *The Mishnah;*. Oxford: Clarendon, 1933. Print.

Demosthenes. "Small Opportunities Are Often the the Beginning of Great Enterprises." *BrainyQuote*. Xplore. Web. 26 Jan. 2014.

Dobson, James C. *Dare to Discipline*. Wheaton, IL: Tyndale House, 1970. Print.

Earl, Doc. "The Heart of the Matter." *Doc Earl: Healing by Design*. Present Doc Earl. Web.

Fill My Cup, Lord. RCA Records, 1969. CD.

Franklin, Aretha, and James Cleveland. *Amazing Grace.* Atlantic, 1972. CD.

Gandhi, Mahatma. "Brainy Quote." *BrainyQuote.* Xplore. Web. 06 Jan. 2014.

Gibbon, Edward. *The Decline and Fall of the Roman Empire.* New York: Modern Library, 1932. Print.

Gould, Leslie. ""Sometimes God Calms the Storm, but Sometimes God Lets the Storm Rage and Calms His Child."" *Goodreads.* Goodreads Inc. Web. 07 Jan. 2014.

Graham, Billy. "The Enduring Classics of Billy Graham (Google EBook)." *Google Books.* Web. 07 Jan. 2014.

Graham, Billy. "Hope for the Troubled Heart: Finding God in the Midst of Pain (Google EBook)." *Google Books.* Web. 07 Jan. 2014.

Greenberg, Peter. "Miracle on the Hudson: What Went Right." *TODAY.com.* NBC News, 17 Jan. 2009. Web. 07 Jan. 2014.

Henry, Patrick. "Patrick Henry Quotes." *ThinkExist.com.* Think Exist. Web.

"Hope for the Troubled Heart: Finding God in the Midst of Pain (Google EBook)." *Google Books.* Web. 07 Jan. 2014.

"Horatius Bonar Quotes." *Horatius Bonar Quotes.* Christian.com. Web. 07 Jan. 2014.

"HubbleSite - Out of the Ordinary…out of This World." *HubbleSite - Out of the Ordinary…out of This World.* NASA. Web. 05 Jan. 2014.

"J. Sidlow Baxter Quotes." *J. Sidlow Baxter Quotes (Author of Baxter's Explore the Book).* Goodreads Inc. Web. 07 Jan. 2014.

Jackson, Mahalia. *Mahalia Jackson, the World's Greatest Gospel Singer.* Columbia, 1955. CD.

Kenyon, Ralph. "Knows and Knows Not." *Xenodochy.com.* 16 Nov. 2009. Web.

Bibliography

"Magnitude 9.1 - OFF THE WEST COAST OF NORTHERN SUMATRA." *Magnitude 9.1 - OFF THE WEST COAST OF NORTHERN SUMATRA*. Web. 12 Jan. 2014.

Martin, Rev. W. "My Father Watches Over Me." *My Father Watches Over Me*. 1910. Vinyl recording.

Maxwell, John C. "Keeping Stress from Becoming Distress." *CFaith.com*. CFaith Ministries. Web.

The Miracle Worker. Dir. Arthur Penn. Perf. Anne Bancroft, Patty Duke, Victor Joy. United Artists, 1962. DVD.

Mote, Edward X. "Solid Rock." *My Hope Is Built on Nothing Less*. Edward Mote. CD.

Olson, Roger E. "Did Karl Barth Really Say "Jesus Loves Me, This I Know....?"" *Roger E Olson*. Web. 12 Jan. 2014.

Parks, Cara. "Darlene Etienne, Haiti Earthquake Survivor 'Miracle,' Makes Full Recovery." *The Huffington Post*. TheHuffingtonPost.com, 11 Jan. 2011. Web. 26 Jan. 2014.

Peale, Dr. Norman V. "You Can If You Think You Can (Google EBook)." *Google Books*. Simon and Schuster. Web. 06 Jan. 2014.

"Popular Poems of Emily Dickinson." *Popular Poems of Emily Dickinson*. Biography Online. Web. 06 Jan. 2014.

"Richard Cecil Quotes." *BrainyQuote*. Xplore. Web. 07 Jan. 2014.

Rockefeller, John D. "How Much Is Enough." *Stewardship Ministries*. Stewardship Ministries, 1 Mar. 2012. Web. 06 Jan. 2014.

Schaeffer, Francis A. *He Is There and He Is Not Silent*. Wheaton, IL: Tyndale House, 1972. Print.

Schnall, Marianne. "An Interview With Maya Angelou." Interview. Web log post. *Psychology Today*. The Guest Room, 17 Feb. 2009. Web.

Shakespeare, William. "Added by Staff." *Quotations Book*. Quotations Book. Web. 06 Jan. 2014.

Shakespeare, William, and William Lyon Phelps. *The Merchant of Venice*. New Haven: Yale UP, 1923. Print.

Spurgeon, Charles. "Christ Crucified." *The Spurgeon Archive*. Web. 12 Jan. 2014.

Steinberg, Jeff. *Masterpiece in Progress*. Green Forest, AR: New Leaf, 1990. Print.

Swindoll, Charles. "Getting Through the Tough Stuff: It's Always Something! (Google EBook)." *Google Books*. Thomas Nelson Inc. Web. 07 Jan. 2014.

Ten, Boom Corrie. *Amazing Love*. Fort Washington, PA: Christian Literature Crusade, 1971. Print.

"We Had a Miracle on 34th Street. I Believe Now We Have Had a Miracle on the Hudson," New York Gov. David Paterson." *CI Blog RSS*. Catholic Ireland. Web. 07 Jan. 2014.

Yancey, Phillip. "Where Is God When It Hurts?" *PhillipYancey.com*. Word Press. Web. 07 Jan. 2014.

www.ingramcontent.com/pod-product-compliance
Lightning Source LLC
LaVergne TN
LVHW041619070426
835507LV00008B/345